Good Dirt

GOOD DIRT

Confessions of a Conservationist

by David E. Morine

Chester, Connecticut

Library of Congress Cataloging-in-Publication Data
Morine, David E.
Good dirt : confessions of a conservationist / by David E. Morine.
— 1st ed.
p. cm.
ISBN 0-87106-444-8
1. Nature conservation—United States. 2. Nature Conservancy (U.S.) I. Title.
QH76.M67 1990
333.7′2—dc20 90-43074
CIP

Manufactured in the United States of America
First Edition/First Printing

To my old friends at the Conservancy:
Stay focused, buy land!

Contents

The reason the eagle can fly so high
is because it takes itself so lightly.

—*Maryann Bassett*

Introduction

CONSERVATION IS MY CHOSEN PROFESSION. From 1972 to 1987 I was in charge of land acquisition for The Nature Conservancy, a nonprofit organization. During that time, we acquired three million acres of land, completed 5,000 projects, and protected 2,000 of America's most significant natural areas. We ran a good business. We raised some money. We saved some land. We had some fun.

When I started with the Conservancy, saving land was a relatively simple business. We'd look around, find some land that we liked, and buy it. Once we had acquired an area, I really believed that it would be protected in perpetuity. I, like most people, had never heard of acid rain, the greenhouse effect, or holes in the ozone layer. We didn't deal in doom and gloom. We bought land.

Today, things are different. Dire predictions seem to be the staple of the conservation movement. Most conservationists are consumed by problems for which there are no simple solutions. What good does it do, for example, to buy a forest unless you can protect it from acid rain? Why save a tidal marsh if it is going to be lost to rising oceans resulting from global warming? Who can worry about a piece of native tallgrass prairie when we are destroying the atmosphere? It is no wonder that so many of today's conservationists seem so somber. They see so many threats to the environment that they can't enjoy being conservationists. For them, humor has become a rare and endangered species.

During my tenure at The Nature Conservancy, we were generally considered to be the most businesslike of the conservation organizations. We probably were. But that didn't mean that we didn't have our share of screw-ups. Any time you undertake a major land deal, something is going to go wrong. When that happens, you can do one of two things: You can get upset, or you can laugh. More often than not, we laughed.

I believe that a large part of the Conservancy's success has been due to the fact that we never took ourselves too seriously. We never let the big issues get us down. We never spent too much time agonizing over the big picture. We attacked the problem of saving significant natural areas one piece at a time.

We weren't naive. We knew we weren't going to save the world, but we thought we could save small and important parts of it. We were focused in our work; we were happy being conservationists.

This collection of stories describes some of my more monumental foul-ups. Most are informative; a few are irreverent, and at least one is totally tasteless. Despite my having been justifiably accused of never letting the facts get in the way of a good story, these stories are, on the whole, true. I hope they will explain a little about land conservation and give conservationists a much-needed lift. With all the doom and gloom being written today, we could use a laugh.

Acknowledgments

I WROTE ONLY about 80 percent of this book. Paul Flint added the other 20 percent. Most of the good stuff is Paul's. Susan Flint critically reviewed each story and saved us from many lapses of judgment. Any good taste in this book is due to Susan. Ruth Morine checked for grammar and punctuation; more important, she provided us with food, drink, and a quiet place to work. My dad bought us a word processor. Jean Miller was always Word Perfect. Will Murray and Dr. Robert Jenkins gave us scientific support. Dan Fales named these stories *Good Dirt,* Mike Dennis made them legal. Ed Cohen sifted through them, and the crew at the Globe Pequot Press shoveled them into a book. Special thanks to Pat Noonan, the Richard King Mellon Foundation, and The Nature Conservancy.

Just Lookin' for Fish

JORDAN'S CAMPS WAS THE NICEST PLACE I have ever been. That was back in the fifties and sixties, before a wave of uncontrolled development swept over the lakes of western Maine. Physically, the camps weren't much: eight rustic little cabins on the south side of Lovewell Pond, just outside of Fryeburg. People didn't go to Jordan's for physical amenities. Reading by kerosene lamps, buying blocks of ice for the refrigerator, cooking on a wood stove, and carrying water half a mile from the spring while fighting off deerflies and mosquitoes were all part of the charm of Jordan's Camps.

My family vacationed at Jordan's from 1946 to 1970. My father always reserved the same cabin, Little Beaver, for the first two weeks in July. He liked going early in July because the long days gave him more time for fishing. Lovewell Pond was loaded with perch, hornpout, pickerel, and, if you were very good and very lucky, smallmouth bass. Catching a bass in Lovewell was a big deal.

The same people came back to Jordan's year after year. Our group consisted of the Garlands from Waltham, the Cunninghams from

Beverly, and the Dohertys from Milton. We were all members of an extended family.

The Reverend Jack Jordan owned the camps. He was too shy and aloof to be part of the family, but he gave the camps their family feeling. Jack Jordan was from Fryeburg. He had inherited the camps from his father and obviously loved them as much as we did.

It was hard to picture him as a minister. Whenever we saw him, he was patching up boats, fixing screens, raking the beach, or even building a couple of new cabins. Although he never asked, everyone would pitch in whenever the Reverend needed help. None of the vacationers seemed to mind working at camp, because they were paying next to nothing in rent. The $20 per week the Reverend charged in 1946 was still only $50 per week by 1970. The Reverend wasn't making much money on the camps, but making money was not the reason he kept them. In a way, we all owned Jordan's Camps.

The Reverend Jordan would often take me with him when he went to scrounge things for the camps. Nothing at Jordan's Camps was new. We'd spend hours rummaging through old houses and barns, and even the Fryeburg Dump, looking for items to furnish the cabins. The Reverend knew everyone. He'd been a big track star at Fryeburg Academy, and much of our scrounging time was spent swapping stories about meets of long ago. The guy who ran the dump had anchored the relay team. That was always an extended stop while they reran the 1930 upset of Gould Academy.

One day while we were driving along, we passed a dead cat. "Uh-oh," said the Reverend. "We can't leave the poor fella like that." He stopped his little Nash and got a burlap bag out of the trunk. He carefully folded the bag and spread it out next to the cat. "Okay, Davey," he said, "you kick the cat, while I hold the bag." I gave the cat a good boot, and in it went.

I didn't feel quite right about kicking an animal, even a dead one, but it didn't bother the Reverend. He shook the cat to the bottom of the bag and twirled it around his head three times. "In the name of the Father," *whoosh,* "the Son," *whoosh,* "and the Holy Ghost," *whoosh.* I watched in amazement as he released the bag and the cat sailed through the trees to its final resting place. The Reverend stood respectfully until we heard a distant plop. "Amen."

When I told my father about the cat and the Reverend's benediction, he chuckled and said, "Jack Jordan is more Mainer than minister."

The Reverend decided to move Jordan's Camps into the twentieth century when we found a bunch of used, but perfectly serviceable, flush toilets out behind the fairgrounds. The manager, a former sprinter for the Academy, said we were welcome to them. The Fryeburg Fair was getting so big and successful that they had built a brand new comfort station.

Everyone at camp was delighted. Block ice, kerosene lamps, wood stoves, and spring water were pleasant reminders of the past, but it was hard to get too nostalgic over a two-holer. The problem was how to dig the eight septic tanks for the new toilets. There was no Environmental Protection Agency back in the fifties, and a septic tank was just a hole in the ground reinforced by railroad ties, but the Reverend couldn't afford to have a contractor come in to dig the holes. His solution was to take a sledge hammer and a crowbar and punch holes deep in the ground where he wanted the tanks. Then, while all the kids in camp were watching, he dropped nickels and dimes and, he claimed, at least one half-dollar, down the holes. We immediately started digging for the money. Within two days, the Reverend had his eight holes, and every kid in camp had unearthed enough change for a sundae at Solari's.

I went with the Reverend to pick up the toilets. He had borrowed a flatbed truck from some lumberjack who had put the shot for the

Academy. On the way home, we were cruising along with our commodes when the Reverend asked me if there was anything wrong. I had to confess that I had a problem. We were about to finish another year at camp, I was almost thirteen, and I still had never caught a bass. Nobody ever came out and said it, but you weren't considered a man at Jordan's until you had caught a bass. Richard Cunningham, who was thirteen, had just landed his first, and even Brian Doherty, my friend Jimmy's little brother who was only nine, had come in the night before with a nice two-pounder. Brian was strutting around camp, bragging on his bass. What made matters worse was that I had hooked a beauty the previous week and lost it. Bobby Garland, who was a great fisherman like his dad, caught my bass two nights later. It still had my jitterbug in its mouth. The whole camp laughed when Bobby came in and presented me with my lure. "Here you go," he said. "Try not to lose it again. Har, har."

Lovewell wasn't a bass pond. Most people who fished Lovewell were looking for perch. There was only one place on the whole pond where you might find a bass. That was a rock outcropping called the Ledge. If you knew what you were doing, and were lucky, you might hook into a bass at the Ledge.

The Reverend told me to relax. "Don't worry, Davey," he said quite confidently. "I'll take you out tonight and we'll catch you a bass. Ayuh." I was very excited. No one had ever seen the Reverend go fishing, but everyone assumed he was a great sportsman. He had three huge bass mounted on the wall of his cabin. They were bigger than anything the Garlands had ever caught, and he claimed they came out of Lovewell.

Right after supper I grabbed my equipment and went down to the Reverend's boat. I waited and waited. All the other boats in the camp were out, but still there was no sign of the Reverend. The sun had almost set before he arrived. He was carrying a big Army-surplus flashlight and a tin can. "Yawl set, Davey?"

"Yessir."

"Well, push 'er out, and we'll get us a bass."

Some of the boats were already coming in as we rowed toward the Ledge. The Reverend had a strong, easy, athletic stroke. He rowed as he must have run. It was almost dark when we reached the buoy that marked the Ledge. I grabbed the anchor, but the Reverend said, "Not yet, Davey." He squinted through his wire-rimmed glasses and carefully lined us up with a tall pine that stood silhouetted above the tree line. When he felt that he had us in exactly the right spot, he said, "Put 'er down, Davey."

He reached into the tin can and brought out the biggest night crawler I had ever seen. He fondled it in his hand and appeared to be tickling its belly. "Ayuh, he's ready. Pass me your hook." I watched as the Reverend carefully wound the hook through the worm. When he was finished, he said, "Drop 'em in, give 'em about eight feet."

I did as instructed. By now it was almost totally dark. The flashlight took me by surprise. It was extremely bright. The Reverend shone it down the line into the water, toward my worm. I thought that this was very strange. "What are you doing, Reverend Jordan?"

He kept staring into the water. "Oh, nawthin. Just lookin' for fish."

Before I had a chance to say anything else, there was a strong jerk on my line. I don't remember the actual fight, but it didn't last very long. The next thing I knew, the Reverend had grabbed the leader and was pulling my bass into the boat. This little fellow would never claim a spot on the Reverend's wall, but it was my first bass.

The whole camp was waiting for us when we came in. There was a big cheer when I proudly held up my fish. At last: I was a man.

When I told my dad about how the Reverend used a flashlight to look for fish, he chuckled again and said we'd better keep that to ourselves. "Why?" I asked him.

"Seems like the Reverend has his own way of fishing," he said.

It took a few years before I fully appreciated what the Reverend had done. Fishing with a flashlight—even to repair the pride of a thirteen-year-old kid—is not universally accepted as sporting. My dad was right. Jack Jordan is more Mainer than minister, and I for one am glad of it.

One Over Our Limit

MY FRIEND RAMSAY FANCIES HIMSELF a real bass man. We met when we were at business school. That was back in the late sixties, at the University of Virginia. Ramsey fished all the time. He had married a local girl whose father had a bass pond right behind the house. Her old man kept it filled with largemouth bass, big lazy lunkers that just lay there waiting to be fed. He'd let Ramsay hook into a couple whenever he came out for a visit. Ramsay loved to catch bass.

After graduation, I had gone to work for a developer of vacation homes. I spent most of my time touring the most beautiful parts of New England, figuring out how to chop them up into lots for A-frames. Business school had warped my values. I'd become consumed with making money. Ramsey had taken a prestigious job with the Boston Consulting Group. Unfortunately for Ramsay, Boston was a long way from his father-in-law's bass pond. When he called me one day, he was desperate. He had tried fishing all over the Northeast, and was convinced that there wasn't a single bass north of the Mason-Dixon Line.

I thought back to Jordan's Camps and remembered how much I

loved to fish. Every night, if it wasn't raining or too windy, we'd row out and try our luck. There weren't any motors on the pond back then. My father had a real rod, but my brother and I used freshly cut saplings with a piece of string and a hook tied to the end. For bait we used worms we brought from home. My dad claimed that Maine fish loved Massachusetts worms. He must have been right, because we always caught a bundle of fish: hornpout, white perch, yellow perch, and even an occasional smallmouth bass. Catching a bass in Lovewell Pond was a big deal. Real bass men didn't fish Lovewell. They went to a secret pond, up toward North Fryeburg.

Sitting in an old wooden boat, listening to the water lap against the side, and watching the sun set into the White Mountains was an experience unto itself, but the real thrill came when Old Tom, the last eagle I've seen in this part of Maine, would burst from a tall pine and dive into a school of perch. When that happened, every boat on the pond would beat its oars to the spot. Your heart would be thumping the whole way, but when you got there it was well worth the effort. The water would be alive with fish. I remember one night we caught forty-three white perch. News of our success, as reported by my father, was printed in the *Arlington Advocate.* Much credit was given to the Massachusetts worms.

The last time my dad and I fished Lovewell Pond was in 1967. By then, our new aluminum boat was powered by a three-horsepower Evinrude, and my sapling rod had been replaced by a fancy spinning outfit. Old Tom was gone, the schools of fish were gone, and the pond was littered with speedboats. We trolled all day and managed to catch three small white perch. Our Massachusetts worms came up wrinkled and neglected. Fishing just wasn't fun anymore.

Then I got the call from Ramsay. He sounded so distraught that I decided I had to help. I told him not to worry, that there was a secret pond just north of Fryeburg that supposedly was loaded with smallmouth bass. I'd only been there a couple of times, but if he knew what he was doing, he'd most likely catch a bass. Meanwhile, I was thinking to myself that this pond might give me a chance to make some money. Given the growth that had taken place around Fryeburg, it must just be ripe for development.

Ramsay was parked outside my door at noon the very next Saturday. He had his canoe tied onto the top of his car and the back was loaded with all kinds of camping and fishing equipment. Our objective was clearly defined by two decals on the back window. One said, "Stop Wishin' and Start Fishin'," the other was the official insignia of the Bass Anglers and Sportsmen's Society, B.A.S.S.

Ramsay made me read aloud from *McClane's Standard Fishing Encyclopedia* as we headed for Fryeburg. The chapter on bass was dogeared and thoroughly annotated. The part he liked best was the section called "Angling Value." It stated: "The smallmouth bass is widely acclaimed as the top trophy of the bass family. The fish is extremely active and usually jumps when hooked. The average smallmouth is not nearly as large as many freshwater fish, but the capture of a four-to-five pounder requires more skill and more patience than the taking of many species of comparable size." Ramsay had me read that part several times.

North of Fryeburg, we left the paved road and headed into the woods. I thought that Ramsay was going to wreck his car as we bounced through a maze of old logging roads. Ramsay hardly slowed down. It was time to "Stop Wishin' and Start Fishin'."

When I finally found the pond, Ramsay insisted that we launch the canoe immediately. He wanted to scout the pond for submerged rocks and logs and other spots where bass might be hiding. I paddled while Ramsay peered at the bottom and tested the water temperature with his official B.A.S.S. thermometer. Except for one new cabin down at the far end, nothing had changed. The pond was still natural and wild.

It reminded me of what Lovewell used to be like when I was a kid. It was a developer's dream.

Ramsay consulted his Solunar Tables and proclaimed that we had exactly one hour and ten minutes before we had to start fishin'. I used that time to walk the shoreline and mark off potential house sites while he fiddled with his equipment. At precisely 7:25 P.M., we hit the water.

Ramsay took complete command. He put me in the bow and told me that we would paddle about thirty yards from shore, trolling a line on each side of the canoe. I tied on a Rapala, an underwater lure that looks like a minnow. Ramsay scoffed at my Rapala. "Overrated," he said. He chose a Tony Accetta Jelly Belly with the Glow Eyes. "When they see these Glow Eyes, they'll be jumping into the canoe."

Within ten minutes, I felt a strong jerk on my line. I looked back and saw a smallmouth leap out of the water. Ramsay was ecstatic. It was the first smallmouth he had ever seen. The fish lived up to McClane's billing: The capture did indeed "require more skill and more patience than the taking of many species of comparable size." Ramsay studied the fish in great detail and carefully photographed it from several angles before releasing it. He was sure that in a matter of minutes he would be posing with one of his own.

Only it didn't happen. My Rapala hooked another beauty, which Ramsay didn't bother to photograph. He was too busy changing lures. His second selection was Bagley's Famous Mud Bug. He lovingly tied it to the end of his line and beamed as he watched it wriggle through the water. "My father-in-law's bass stand in line to get a shot at this baby," he told me.

By nine o'clock, the Rapala had scored again, but the Mud Bug had lured only one fish, and it got away. The real bugs were getting bad and I was ready to quit, but Ramsay insisted we make one last run.

Since the water was calm, Ramsay decided to switch to a surface lure. He rummaged through several layers of his tackle box and finally settled upon Fred Arbogast's classic Double-Lobed Lip Jitterbug. This particular model had the markings of a green frog and two sets of treble hooks.

It was totally dark by the time we started back to camp. We were each trailing about twenty-five yards of line when Ramsay announced he had a strike. We couldn't see the Jitterbug, but we heard two splashes which we assumed were the customary jumps of a small-mouth bass. I reeled in my line and grabbed the net.

Ramsay was positive he had a big one. "Let's hear it for Fred Arbogast! This could be a new school and pool! This mother's really jumping!" Then there was a dramatic change in his voice. "Hey," he said anxiously, "something's wrong here." He was holding the rod vertically over his head, reeling frantically.

"Ramsay! Get your rod down! You're going to lose him if he comes up!"

"Comes up? He's already up! He's someplace over my head!"

"What?"

At that moment, a large white object came soaring over the canoe and slammed into the water. Ramsay was still playing it for all he was worth. McClane would have been very proud. "Get the light!" Ramsay screamed. "Get the light!"

"What light?"

"The one in my tackle box!"

I leaned back, but I couldn't reach his tackle box. By this time, Ramsay's "fish" had taken off again. It circled the canoe and crashed into the woods.

"Ramsay," I said, "you must have caught a bird. Hold the line, and I'll paddle us to shore."

"The hell with that. I'm cutting this line, before whatever it is comes back."

I started to protest, but Ramsay cut the line before I could say anything. We could hear the bird in the woods, trying to shake the Jitterbug. "Let's get back to camp," Ramsay said. He was not pleased.

Memories of Old Tom, fishing on Lovewell, came back to me. Could Ramsay possibly have hooked an eagle? "Wait a minute," I said. "We can't leave that bird. It might be an eagle."

"Whatever it is, it's big, and it's mean," Ramsay replied. "Besides, what chance do we have of finding it in the dark?"

We heard the tinkle of hooks as the bird continued to try to free itself. It was only a few hundred feet away. "I'll tell you what," I said. "Let's go down to that cabin and see if they have some flashlights. Maybe there are some kids there who will help us."

We paddled down and introduced ourselves to Dick and Pat de La Chapelle and their four children. The de La Chapelles couldn't believe that Ramsay had caught a bird. The kids quickly ran off to find it. We stumbled along the shore behind them. After half an hour, we had found nothing. We were just about to give up when we heard the sound of hooks tinkling under a bush. I turned the light toward the sound and saw two huge brown eyes glaring at me. The bird was a barred owl. Its beak and talons were locked together by the treble hooks. The line was hanging from the branch of a tree. The owl must have tried to gain a perch and fallen into the bush.

One of the kids started toward it. Dick de La Chapelle pulled him back. "Watch it! If that bird gets excited, you could lose an eye."

He was right; the combination of beak, talons, and hooks made the owl very dangerous. "Let's see if we can get it back to the cabin where we can take a good look at it," I said. I took off my jacket, one of those heavy, red-and-black Woolrich shirts, and threw it over the owl.

Back at the cabin, I placed the bird on the picnic table, next to Dick de La Chapelle's big kerosene lantern. I gingerly removed the jacket. The bird lay there, studying me with its huge brown eyes. Now that I had more light, I could see that it had hit the lure with its right talon, where two hooks were embedded. Then, in its efforts to free itself, it had put a hook into its left talon and another into its beak.

"Ramsay," I said. "Get in here and help me clean your fish."

Ramsay was standing back with the de La Chapelles. Dick was still trying to restrain his curious kids. "You've got to be kidding," Ramsay said.

"Come on, it's just a bird."

"That's not just a bird; that's a big bird, with a big beak, big talons, and big hooks."

I knew he was right, but I had to try to free this bird, and to do that, I needed Ramsay's help. "Come on. All you have to do is hold the wings and consult. I'll do the cutting."

The idea of consulting must have appealed to Ramsay. He stepped forward and grabbed the owl by both wings. I took a pair of pliers and went to work. I had no idea what the owl might do when I freed its beak and talons. "Ramsay," I said, "if he starts to attack me, let him go."

"Don't worry" was all Ramsay said. I could see the sweat on his brow and felt a bead trickling down my own nose.

Remarkably, the bird just lay there. It must have been in shock. As I removed the final hook, I no longer felt like a developer. I felt like John J. Audubon, Izaak Walton, and Aldo Leopold all rolled into one.

"Okay, Ramsay, nice going," I told him. "Your consulting job is over."

Ramsay looked very relieved as he moved back to where the de La Chapelles were standing. I wrapped the bird back into my jacket, picked it up, and laid it on the dock. Swaddled in my Woolrich with only its head showing, it looked like a baby with extra big eyes and a funny haircut. "Ramsay, quick, take a picture," I said. "You can send it to your father-in-law. Show him what a real smallmouth looks like." Ramsay got one shot of his owl before it wriggled itself free, defecated on my jacket, and flew into the night.

We fished again the next morning. Instead of thinking about ways to develop the pond, I found myself thinking about ways to protect it. All Ramsay was thinking about was fish. He had switched to his ultimate weapon, the Sidewinder, made by the Acme Tackle Company. My Rapala caught one more nice bass, but the Sidewinder came up empty. No fish, no birds, no nothing.

I was in high spirits during the drive back to Boston. This trip had convinced me that I was not cut out to be a developer. I didn't want to exploit these beautiful places. What I really wanted to do was to protect them. I suggested to Ramsay that we come back again the next weekend. He was noncommittal. He seemed to have lost interest in discussing the angling value of smallmouth bass.

I called Ramsay at his office a few days later. I wanted to see if we were going fishing and tell him that I was looking for a job in conservation. I planned to give his owl full credit. Ramsay's secretary told me that he was out of town and wouldn't be back until the following week. He was on some personal business. He had gone to see his father-in-law in Virginia.

Welcome to the Family

WHEN I STARTED WITH THE NATURE CONSERVANCY in January of 1972, we had forty-eight full-time employees. We were a family. The members of the board of governors were the parents. They gave us their time, their wisdom, their wealth; they constantly pushed us to reach our potential. Pat Noonan, the Conservancy's young and energetic director of operations, was the big brother—protective, supportive, understanding, and continually leading the way. Raised in this happy atmosphere, it was no wonder that the rest of us grew up as bright, happy, energetic, clean-cut conservationists.

Every Friday afternoon, Pat hosted an informal "Happy Hour" in our conference room. He'd personally buy a couple of cases of beer, and while attendance wasn't mandatory, everyone who was in town always showed up. These get-togethers would often last far into the evening. Pat would set the tone and direction by highlighting what we'd accomplished that week. He made sure each individual knew that he or she was playing an important role in the success of the Conservancy.

"Miriam wrote the check that saved 1,500 acres of environmentally sensitive tidal marsh in Georgia," he'd announce. "Thank you, Miriam." There was enthusiastic applause. Miriam would flush, overcome with the significance of her deed.

"Josephine opened the envelope that contained the donation that allowed Miriam to write the check," Pat would continue. More applause. "What'd we do today, Jo?" he'd ask, knowing the answer.

"Everyone we could, and the good ones twice," Jo would chime. "We got 122 new members this week." Jo loved opening those envelopes and counting those checks.

"We *can* do 'em twice because Mirdza made the labels for all those new members," Pat would say. Clap, clap, clap.

Mirdza was a very precise Latvian who pounded proudly on the Addressograph for eight hours a day. "Dat vas vun hundert und tventy-eight, Pott, vich is da best vee haff ever done." More clap, clap, clap.

Fitzie, our controller, had known Pat since they were kids. He loved to needle him. "Say, buddy boy," he'd ask accusingly, "do those 128 new members know that their hard-earned money is being used to send you and these other bozos all over the country? You guys have already busted the travel budget."

Unfazed, Pat would respond, "Fitzie, I'm sure all of our new members would like to hear this from you directly. We're gonna send you out to tell them." Much laughter. Everyone knew that Fitzie got sick just looking at an airplane.

Pat saved his best for those of us who were doing the deals. "Greg just completed a 120-acre addition to the Blackwater Refuge." With that, he'd hold up the article from a local newspaper as proof that he wasn't making it up. "Here, he even got his picture in the paper." Pat would circulate the paper. And there would be Greg, accepting a deed from an eleemosynary old couple, with some official from the U.S. Fish and Wildlife Service flashing his pearly whites. "As usual, Greg's wearing his photo shirt." Much hilarity. Greg always wore the same striped shirt whenever he thought he was going to have his picture taken. He claimed that the stripes showed up better in a photo. He had learned that in college. "Dress for the Press" must have been a required course at Chapel Hill.

"We're going to send this picture down to the *Rocky Mount Observer,*" Pat would add. "Let the folks back home know that Greg's not up here sleeping." The amazing thing was that Pat would actually do it. A few weeks later, Greg would bring in a copy of the *Observer.* There would be his picture on the front page, captioned, "Local Boy Saves Land in Maryland." The article would talk about Greg, his being a graduate of UNC, his parents, his grandparents, the Conservancy, and anything else the *Observer* felt was newsworthy. What the article wouldn't say was that Pat had set the whole deal up, that it had been almost impossible for Greg to fail. Greg would know it. We'd all know it. But it wouldn't matter. Once you joined the family, Pat, like any good big brother, did his level best to make sure you didn't fail.

Everything was going fine until 1973, when the board of governors charged the staff with developing our first long-range plan. Pat's summaries of what we had accomplished each week were no longer sufficient. The board wanted to know what we were going to accomplish over the next five years.

We'd still spend Friday evenings sitting around the conference table, drinking Pat's beer, but rather than rehashing the glories of the past, we were debating the future. Conviviality began to give way to acrimony. Dr. Robert Jenkins, the Conservancy's chief scientist, had a different vision than the rest of us. He wasn't focused solely on buying land. He maintained that the mission of The Nature Conservancy was the preservation of biotic diversity.

Most of us did not fully understand, or much care about, the concept of biotic diversity. We were MBAs and lawyers, not scientists. Conservation was a business, and most of us saw the aim of that business as buying land. We were looking for deals, not diversity. What difference did it make what we bought as long as it wasn't developed and was applauded by the local press?

This attitude incensed Dr. Bob. "Noah's Ark!" he'd scream, pounding his big fist onto the table. "Think of Noah's Ark. We need two of every kind. Our mission is the preservation of biotic diversity, not just buying land."

We'd look to Pat for guidance. He'd sit back and listen to the debate.

By 1974, we had managed to develop a long-range plan that we felt would make the Conservancy the preeminent land conservation organization in America. It divided the country into four regions. These regions would be the Conservancy's second generation. Each region was to be a family unto itself. Regional directors in turn were charged with establishing self-funding programs in every state within their regions. The state offices would be the third generation within the Conservancy. They would carry the Conservancy's philosophy of "conservation through private action" into the eighties. At Pat's insistence, Dr. Bob wrote the preamble to the plan. It stated boldly that the Conservancy's mission was "the preservation of biotic diversity." Few of us bothered to read the preamble.

We presented the plan at the 1974 annual conference. Our state chapters and local committees, which up to now had consisted solely of volunteers, seized upon the idea of having their own full-time, paid staff directors. They couldn't wait to hire someone.

This was not exactly what most of us had had in mind. Although no one came right out and said it, to us MBAs and lawyers, the idea was to staff the regions with new Pat Noonans, and then have them do the same for the states. That was going to take time, but we didn't have time. The chapters and committees wanted to hire directors as soon as they raised the funds. Our current staff couldn't fill the demand. Pat knew that the only way the national office could retain control was to find some good people, fast. He also knew that we had no training program, no job descriptions, and no recruiters, nor were we offering enough money to attract anyone with business experience. We'd have to gamble.

Our first gamble was when we hired a Vietnam vet as the executive director of one of our oldest and most conservative chapters. This guy made us nervous. He didn't look like us, he didn't act like us, and he wasn't the standard vet. But he did have two principal qualifications: He wanted to get close to nature, and he was willing to accept the pittance we were paying state directors.

Pat asked the chapter chairman, a distinguished professor and community leader, to personally meet the new director's plane. The chairman called Pat from the airport. He was not happy. When the vet got off the plane, he had hair down to his shoulders, was wearing fatigues, was barefoot, and was loaded. "Give him a chance," urged Pat. "He's had a tough time. I'm sure he'll come around. He wants to get close to nature."

Pat flew out to meet with the new director. The vet reaffirmed his desire to get close to nature. Pat said that was nice. He advised him to get his hair cut, to wear a coat and tie, to buy a pair of shoes, and to drink in moderation, especially around board members. Pat's advice was ignored. The vet showed up for his first field trip with the membership shoeless, disheveled, and carrying a six-pack. The only person who seemed to find him attractive was the comely and somewhat rebellious daughter of one of the wealthier board members. Within a week she had moved in with him. Her family was understandably upset. Pat was summoned to a special meeting of the chapter board. Getting close to nature was one thing; getting close to a board member's daughter was something else. Still shoeless, the vet was sent packing from the Conservancy.

The chapter then proceeded to ignore the national offices and hired their own man, a nice young guy from an old and very wealthy local family. He looked right, he acted right, he knew all the right people, but it soon became obvious that he would never be another Pat Noonan. He felt awkward asking people he knew for land and money.

Contrary to the orderly growth we envisioned in the five-year plan, other chapters and committees began hiring their own people. Our regional offices were caught in the middle; the national office was forced to ignore the second generation and try to control the third. Most of these people looked right and acted right, but they weren't doing the job. We couldn't figure out why they failed, but when they failed, it created a lot of tension within the family.

Many a Friday evening was spent trying to determine what it took to be a good state director. The meetings became more and more acrimonious. Much of the support staff, like Miriam, Jo, and Mirdza, stopped coming. Fitzie would slip out early. Dr. Bob spent hours proselytizing about biotic diversity, while the MBAs and lawyers agonized over what it took to be a good state director. None of us had an answer. I drew up the six characteristics I thought we needed in a state director. They were: a historical perspective, a philosophical outlook, a good financial background, a lot of common sense, a sense of humor, and a spiritual commitment. What they added up to sounded a lot like Pat. We printed them up and put them in our new Employee's Manual. They didn't mean a thing. These were characteristics that everybody wanted in any employee. We'd look to Pat for guidance. He'd sit back and pass out more beers.

In the fall of '76, Brad Northrup and I were summoned to Pat's office. Brad had started at the Conservancy just before me and was now being groomed for the new position of director of personnel and administration. From the look in Pat's eyes we sensed we had a problem, but Pat was his usual jovial self. Being negative was not part of Pat's makeup. Pat felt that everything could be presented in a positive light if you just talked around it long enough.

"Good news!" Pat said. "I've got a great trip planned for you guys this weekend." Brad and I looked at each other. Weekend trips were never good news.

Pat wanted us to attend the annual meeting of one of our more obscure committees. There was nothing unusual about headquarters staff attending the annual meeting of a chapter or committee. Annual meetings were our chance to thank the volunteers for all they had done. We would pump them up by giving them a slide show highlighting the major natural areas the Conservancy had saved across the country.

What was unusual was that Pat wanted two of us to go to the meeting of this relatively small and inactive group. Two of us would put a serious crimp in Fitzie's travel budget. "Why do you want both of us to go?" Brad asked.

Pat explained why. "This is a very important meeting," he said, looking quite serious. "The state has proposed the creation of a major park surrounding the preserve managed by this committee. They want our endorsement. I want you guys to make sure they get it. Dr. Bob says that getting the state governments involved is key to his blueprint for preserving biotic diversity."

"But what do the local people think?" I asked.

"They're wonderful people, long-term supporters, and we have to start paying more attention to them. Some of them might have a slight conflict of interest." Ah, now it was clear. The board was rebelling.

"For example?" Brad asked.

"Well, one of the members owns a beautiful motel," Pat said. "She's afraid that if the state puts in a lot of public campsites, she'll lose business."

"Is that all?" Brad asked.

"That's about it," Pat said matter-of-factly. Then he added, almost as an afterthought, "But there are a couple of board members who have large tracts of land and don't want the state taking their property. Then, of course, there's our major donor who owns a sawmill and is convinced the park will dry up his supply of timber."

"Pat!" I exclaimed incredulously. "There can't be more than half a dozen members on that board. Is anyone in favor of this park?"

"There must be a couple. I'm sure you'll be able to turn them around. And don't worry, their new executive director will be right with you."

"New executive director?" Brad's voice went up an octave. "What new executive director? Those guys spend half their time recycling paper clips. How can they afford a new director?"

"They're all excited," Pat said. "They've coughed up the dough. He's some young hotshot from Madison Avenue. He wanted out of the rat race. The chairman told me that they were lucky to get him. Help him out. Welcome him into the family."

We got our tickets. Brad called the new director. "He might be okay," he told me. "He's originally from that area. He's going to meet us at the airport."

Our plane got in at five on Friday afternoon. The annual meeting started at six. A field trip through the preserve was scheduled for the next morning, followed by a picnic lunch. Brad and I would have to stay over Saturday night—Fitzie insisted that we get the weekend rates.

We scanned the crowd meeting our flight. We were expecting somebody like us, a clean-cut, rosy-cheeked guy wearing a blue blazer, white shirt, chino pants and Weejuns. He wasn't there. We scoured the airport. We finally found our man in the Hangar Club. He was sitting at the bar sipping a Scotch and water, a cigarette dangling from his lip. His stylishly long hair, tailor-made suit, silk tie, and Gucci loafers were all Madison Avenue. He looked very comfortable.

The new director recognized us immediately. The oak leaf patch on Brad's rucksack must have given us away. He acknowledged our arrival with a wave to the bartender. "Hey, Pete, set these boys up, and how about another one for me."

We normally abstained from drinking before meetings, but the new director hadn't left us much choice. We each ordered a draft, the preferred beverage of Conservancy staff.

The new director was apologetic. "Gee, I'm sorry things look so bleak."

Brad pulled out his notes for the meeting. "No, no, I'm sure we'll be able to turn these people around."

"What people?" the new director said. "This place is dead. It doesn't pick up until Happy Hour." He checked his Rolex. "It starts at six. Two for one, all drinks. It's a great deal."

Brad looked at me for help.

"Ah, we were talking about the annual meeting," I said. "Doesn't that start at six?"

"Don't worry, we've got plenty of time. They'll be flapping their gums over that park issue all night."

"Don't you think we should be there pushing for the park?" Brad asked.

"Naaah," said the new director, lighting up another cigarette. "These meetings are a waste of time. If the state wants a park, they'll make a park. Who cares what we think. I'm not getting paid enough to worry about it."

I looked at Brad. Brad looked at me. We didn't like this guy. "Well, we care," I said. "Let's get to the meeting." We grabbed our rucksacks and headed outside. The new director gulped his drink and followed reluctantly.

The meeting was being held at an old lodge overlooking the lake. The lake was to be the centerpiece of the proposed park. When we walked in, the debate was raging. A couple of dozen people were all clamoring to make their points, for or against the park. The chairman looked relieved to see us. The meeting had gotten out of hand. He banged his gavel. "Ah, at last. Two representatives from headquarters. Let's hear what the Conservancy is up to in other parts of the country."

"Good luck," said the new director. "I'll see you in the tap room."

Brad quickly set up the slide show and took the membership on a tour of our major preserves. He was careful to stress how we were working with state governments. Then I talked about our five-year plan and our effort to leverage our private resources by serving as a catalyst for public funding. As soon as I was through, the chairman opened the floor to questions. There weren't any. Some guy in the back jumped up. "Let's get on with it. I move we vote down this damn park." There was a murmur of agreement.

I leaped to my feet. Pat had instructed us not to come back without an endorsement. "We're not leaving here without a positive resolution," I told the committee. "The Nature Conservancy strongly favors the creation of state parks. We don't care how you word the resolution, just so long as it's positive."

After another two hours of acrimonious debate, the committee finally voted in favor of a watered-down, conditional, contingent, begrudging, cantankerous resolution supporting the park. It called for strictly limiting public access and acquiring land only from willing sellers; it strongly supported traditional uses such as timbering and mining, and it recommended no more than one motel. But, all things considered, it was an endorsement.

The meeting adjourned and the committee headed for the tap room. By the time Brad and I packed up the slide show, the only seats left were next to the new director. "How'd it go?" he inquired cheerfully.

"Fine, no thanks to you." I was a little short, since we'd just spent two hours doing his job.

The new director sensed our displeasure. "Say, how'd you guys like to go sailing tomorrow? I just got a good deal on a twenty-six-foot O'Day. I'd like to show you the lake."

"We're hiking the preserve with the committee tomorrow," Brad told him. "Aren't you going?"

"Naaah. I've already seen the preserve."

That did it. I thought Brad was going to pop him. Here we were, giving up our weekends to attend his meeting, and he was going sailing. "Let's get out of here," said Brad.

"Right. That was a long meeting," agreed the director. "Let me take you to the motel. It's not the Plaza, but I got you a room for nothing."

Brad and I didn't have much to say during the ride. The new director did all the talking. He told us all about the deals he had gotten on his boat, suits, shoes, cameras, and watches. He pulled up in front of the motel. "Sure you won't change your mind about sailing? It'll be a lot more fun than tromping through the woods."

"We're not here to have fun," I said self-righteously. "We're here to save some land."

"Yeah, well, if you ever need a Nikon, I can get you a great deal." Off he went.

On Monday morning, we presented our patchwork resolution to Pat. We told him it wasn't much, but it was the best we could do. We told him that we'd had to overcome tremendous opposition, that the new director wasn't any help, that he didn't fit the Conservancy's image, that he'd never make it. "Give him a chance," said Pat. "I'm sure he'll come around. He's working on a big project."

A few months later, at the Friday afternoon get-together, the conference room was packed. Pat had indicated that there would be a major announcement. After dutifully acknowledging the good work of Miriam, Jo, Mirdza, and several others, Pat announced the creation of the new state park. He gave Brad and me full credit. "Had Brad and Dave not pushed through this resolution," Pat told the staff, "the state never would have approved the park." Of course that wasn't true, but everybody clapped.

Then Pat announced that the new director had just obtained an easement over 25,000 acres of ponds and streams and virgin forest within the park. The owner had agreed that he, his family, his heirs and assignees would never develop the property. It was the largest conservation easement we'd ever gotten. This donation had been made by one of the most prominent families in America. Pat held up a copy of the *New York Times.* There was a picture of the new director, pumping hands with the landowner. The governor was standing between them, beaming. There was much applause. Even Dr. Bob approved. "Bigger is better," he said. "At last, we're beginning to relate our land acquisition efforts to the preservation of biotic diversity."

Brad grabbed the paper from Pat. We all huddled over the picture. People wanted to know which one was the director. All three appeared far too smooth to work for the Conservancy. Fitzie looked at the picture and said to Greg, "Buddy boy, stuff that 'dress for success' baloney they taught you at UNC. Here's some guys with some real threads."

Later, Brad and I took Pat aside. "Pat," I said, "how did you set this guy up? He doesn't look like us, and he doesn't act like us. He won't even hike his own preserve."

"I didn't," said Pat. "He did it on his own. He knows how to get a deal."

"Impossible!" said Brad.

"Diversity, gentlemen; think diversity. Business is like nature. We don't want to grow into an organization where everybody looks alike, acts alike, and thinks alike. That's the first step toward extinction. We have to be able to adapt to different environments. We live on deals, so what we need are people who like to get a good deal." Pat paused and sipped his beer. "You guys should listen to the Doc. You might learn something."

Going for the Touchdown

EVERYONE AT THE NATURE CONSERVANCY has a favorite project. Mine is the Pascagoula. I favor the Pascagoula because it represents a lot of firsts for the Conservancy. It was the first major project we did in Mississippi. It was the largest appropriation we had ever worked through a state government. It was the start of our ongoing effort to preserve a viable system of bottomland hardwoods. And, most importantly, from my point of view, it was the first time that I was able to emerge from under the long and distinguished, if somewhat stocky, shadow of Pat Noonan.

Pat has always been, and still is, the best dealmaker in land conservation. He has single-handedly saved more significant natural areas than anyone else I know. He is the standard against whom everyone in land conservation must be judged.

When Pat became president of the Conservancy in 1974, he recognized that his primary responsibility would be to raise money and that he would no longer be personally able to direct major projects. He appointed me director of land acquisition. "Your job," he stated, "is to do a bigger and better project than we have ever done before."

Following Pat was no easy task. During the first six months of his presidency, he cleaned off his desk by engineering the donation of 50,000 acres in the Great Dismal Swamp from the Union Camp Corporation; buying Parramore Island, the largest of the Virginia barrier islands, for $1.6 million; and working with then-Governor Jimmy Carter to protect a large stretch of the Chattahoochee River. "There," Pat said as we were flying home from the dedication ceremony in Atlanta, "that cleans out the pipeline. Now I can start raising money while you find our next major project."

Today, thanks to our system of state heritage programs, we've identified habitats for just about every endangered species in the United States. We have all of the significant natural areas inventoried. We know exactly what land we want to protect, and why. Back in 1974, we didn't have this information. Most of our major projects came in over the transom. We used to profess that "haphazard conservation is no better than haphazard development," but we seldom were able to practice what we preached. If it was big and wet, and we thought we could raise the money, we'd buy it. Common sense and expediency were the two most important criteria in our selection process.

On my first day as director of land acquisition, I was on the phone, calling our contacts in New England. I'm from Massachusetts, and I knew that there was growing support for conservation in the Northeast. Common sense told me that's where I would find our next major project.

I was hoping for some good news from the Northeast when a retired attorney who was volunteering at the Conservancy told me about a 42,000-acre swamp along the Pascagoula River, in Mississippi. "It's been owned for years by four families from Laurel," he said. "Some of the kids would rather have money than land. It's one of the last great undisturbed river swamps left in the country. You could probably get the whole thing for around $15 million. You should have a look at it."

Yeah, right, I thought. What were the odds of us doing a major project in Mississippi? We didn't know anybody in Mississippi. We had never done a thing in Mississippi. Of all the states in the Southeast, Mississippi had shown the least interest in acquiring land for conservation. When Pat's good friend from Georgia, Governor Carter, hosted a seminar to introduce the Conservancy to all the conservation agencies in the Southeast, Mississippi was the only state that failed to attend. Mississippi, America's perennial poorest state, was much more interested in development than in conservation. There was no chance of my making my reputation in Mississippi.

I immediately forgot about the Pascagoula and started redialing my contacts in Boston. All they wanted to know was how Pat was doing and when he was going to come up and do a project with them. I told them Pat was no longer directly involved in projects and that they would be dealing with me. Invariably, that was the end of the conversation. After a few weeks, I was getting worried.

Then my phone rang. Some guy named Avery Wood was calling from Jackson, Mississippi. He wanted to talk to the person in charge of land acquisition. His accent was so thick I could hardly understand him. I finally figured out that he was the new director of the Mississippi Game and Fish Department. He wanted me to come down and meet with him. He claimed he "wanted to create the best wildlife management program in America."

I was skeptical, but I had no place else to go. And, finally, someone was willing to talk to me instead of Pat. I went to the dead-project file and retrieved the few notes I had taken on the Pascagoula. All they said were, "42K acres. Finest river swamp in S.E. Kids want $. Pascagoula Hdwd. Co. For sale at $15 million?" This was the sum total of our conservation efforts in Mississippi.

It was a cold November day when I got off the plane in Jackson. The chill in the air surprised me. It had never occurred to me that

Mississippi might be cold. My only impressions of Mississippi came from Hollywood and the press. Mississippi was a hot place, a place that didn't like strangers, especially from the North. I smiled nervously at the burly state trooper who was eyeing the passengers coming off the plane. He reminded me of the pictures of troopers in my college yearbook, the ones who were shown pounding my classmates over the head. Amherst had sent a delegation to Mississippi during the civil rights protest. They were lucky to get back alive.

Fortunately, Avery was there to meet me. He was pacing up and down, puffing on a cigarette. His steel-rimmed glasses and shaggy, prematurely gray hair didn't make him look like the self-proclaimed best damn duck hunter in all of Mississippi. He loaded me into an official state vehicle and drove me downtown to his office. The speedometer seldom dipped below ninety. Our conversation kept pace. Avery's country-boy manners camouflaged a very quick mind that was continually popping off ideas. He wanted to learn everything I knew as quickly as he could.

Avery's office was on the eighth floor of the Robert E. Lee Hotel. The state had purchased this ancient edifice and converted it into an office building. The conversion had been minimal. Except for the furniture, Avery's office still looked like an old hotel room.

Avery's dream was to save Mississippi for the sportsman. He felt that the state, in its frantic efforts to shed its Ku Klux Klan image and attract new industry, was destroying its best business: game and fish. He produced figures showing that, out of a population of roughly two million, more than 600,000 Mississippians bought licenses to hunt and fish. He reached into this closet and pulled out a big cardboard graph. One axis was labeled "Sportsmen"; the other, "Dollars Spent."

"Just take a look at this here graph," Avery said, waving his cigarette in the air. "Outdoor recreation generates $150 million in bidness every year. That there bidness pumps over $7 million of unsolicited tax revenue into the general fund. If we're gonna be bringin' people in from out of state, we oughta be bringin' 'em in to enjoy our natural resources, not to destroy 'em. Those boys over in the legislature want to make Mississippi just like everyplace else. Hail, when it comes to outdoor recreation, we're the leaders."

I was beginning to regret this trip. What was this guy talking about? Game and fish as a business? I didn't come all the way to Mississippi to talk about hunting and fishing "bidness." I came to talk about conservation.

"The problem with Mississippi," he continued, "is that it takes its natural heritage for granted. We assume we got an infinite supply of land. Well, lemme tell ya, that ain't the case."

By now, Avery seemed to have forgotten that I was even there. He railed at the fact that the state owned only a paltry 20,000 acres that were dedicated to game management. The bulk of the game and fish program was run on leased lands. "Them lands ain't gonna be there forever," he exclaimed. "When development comes—and it's gonna come—people ain't gonna let the state use these lands. They're gonna lease 'em to private hunt clubs, or sell 'em for more development. The average guy, the millworker who's been buyin' his license and registrin' his boat every year, he's gonna be locked out. We gotta set up a system of wildlife management areas that are owned by the state. We gotta protect our best bidness. We gotta save Mississippi for the sportsman!"

Avery took his graph and, in disgust, scaled it into the bathroom. He collapsed into his chair and studied me.

Finally it dawned on me that Avery might be on to something. I began to see the connection between the game and fish business and conservation. If you were protecting land for game, you were also protecting it for non-game species. If the Conservancy could tie into the states' game and fish business, we could save a lot of significant natural areas.

Pat Noonan had already come to the conclusion that the best way to move conservation forward was to get the states more involved. He knew that less than one-half of one percent of philanthropic giving went to conservation. It would take conservation years to catch up with more established charities in religion, health, and education. The best natural areas would be long gone by then. Even if we could catch up, it was doubtful that there was enough private money to get the job done.

Under Pat's leadership, the Conservancy's new strategy was to use private funds as a catalyst to stimulate public funding for conservation. We had initiated a program with the federal government, but many members of our board were hesitant to bet all our chips on the Feds. The Feds were too fickle. We had made some real progress under Nixon, but he was gone, and who knew what Ford would do. Historically, conservation had been an easy target for budget cuts. As lawmakers were quick to say, "Birds don't vote."

The best way to secure our public-land protection effort was to buffer our federal program with individual state programs. The big question was, how could we sell conservation to the states? And here was Avery, giving me the answer. The states had to buy land to protect an existing and very profitable business, the game and fish business. This was the genius of Avery's plan. What made it especially attractive to me was that it was coming from Mississippi. Mississippi was perceived as the last in everything. If suddenly it emerged with the best wildlife heritage program, other game and fish departments would have to take notice.

"Avery," I said with genuine awe, "you've got it figured out. Sportsmen should be America's best conservationists. But how do we bridge the gap? How do we start buying natural areas for game and fish?"

Avery sat up. He knew he had me hooked. "Now let me tell ya," he said, smiling. "I've set up this here committee, the Wildlife Heritage Committee, and these boys got the wherewithal to make things happen, ya know what I mean?"

I didn't, but I nodded knowingly.

"Now, these boys, they ain't gonna believe me when I tell 'em we got a problem, 'cause I'm just a country boy. So we'll bring you in, and tell 'em you're the expert."

"Expert?" I protested. "Me? I'm no expert. I'm from Boston. What do I know about hunting and fishing?"

Avery looked at me as if I were a dumb younger brother. "Bubba," he said, "you come in here lookin' Ivy League and throwin' out all those big words, they gonna believe you. An expert ain't nothin' but a regular guy that's a long way from home. With that Boston accent, these boys are gonna know you're a long way from home."

"But what will I tell them?"

"Just give 'em the same facts that I gave you." He got up and went into the bathroom. "Here," he said, coming back with his graph. "Use this. Make it sound like you learned this stuff at MIT."

"Avery, that's a start, but it's not going to do it. You can talk about conservation until you're blue in the face, but people don't respond until they can get their hands into the dirt. We have to give them a project. What do you know about the Pascagoula?"

Avery's eyes lit up. "That swamp's got some of the best huntin' and fishin' in the state. But it's owned by some folks in Laurel. It's never been open to the general public."

"What if I told you we could buy it for $15 million?"

"Fifteen million dollars?" Avery fell back into his seat. "How the hail we gonna raise $15 million?"

"I thought you said these boys had wherewithal. How are you going to create the best wildlife management system in America if you can't raise $15 million?"

Avery regained his feet and looked at his watch. "Bubba, it's time we had ourselves a drink."

The following Monday, at the Conservancy's weekly staff meeting, I described Avery, the Wildlife Management Committee, the concept of game and fish as a business that could help conservation, and our plan to undertake a major project in Mississippi. Most of the staff thought I was crazy. "Yeah, right," they said. "What are the odds of us doing a major project in Mississippi? We have no contact in Mississippi. Nothing ever gets done in Mississippi. Let's not get sidetracked with these game and fish people. You're wasting your time in Mississippi."

As usual, Pat didn't weigh in until he had heard what everyone else had to say. "Game and fish as a business is an interesting concept. Only a handful of people understand biotic diversity, less than four million people support conservation, but there are over twenty million sportsmen. If we want to raise some real money, we've got to expand our base of support. Dave, do you really think we have a chance of doing something in Mississippi?"

"Well, Pat, this guy Avery Wood might be crazy enough to pull if off. I'll know more after I meet with this Wildlife Heritage Committee."

"I guess we can afford another plane ticket to Jackson. Go ahead. Just don't tell Fitzie."

I was the guest expert at the next meeting of the Wildlife Heritage Committee. The meeting was held at the old Robert E. Lee Hotel. The conference room consisted of two former hotel rooms that had been joined together. The result was one long, narrow chamber with a bathroom at each end. The carpeting was threadbare and there was a gap in the middle where the wall had been removed. The mismatched chairs around the conference table looked as if they had been picked up at a Goodwill sale. The protection of Mississippi's wildlife heritage would have to evolve from these humble origins.

The nine committee members looked like something straight out of Tennessee Williams. They were all middle-aged men. They all brandished big, black cigars. Those with a full head of hair had it slicked back into a modified ducktail. Those without, had what was left cropped close, Marine-style. Even though it was winter, their suits were florid. There was much guffawing and backslapping before the meeting. As a guest, I sat demurely in a corner while Avery did his politicking. The room was filled with deep Southern drawls. I couldn't understand most of what was being said.

Three of the members were from the Mississippi State Senate, three were from the House, and three were prominent citizens appointed by the governor. Easily the most prominent of all was Coach John Vaught, the winningest coach in Ole Miss history. He was a living legend, the man who had brought the Rebels to eighteen consecutive bowls. Not surprisingly, the pre-meeting chatter centered around the coach.

From what I could make of the conversation, he was telling the members about last year's victory over Tennessee. The coach had come out of retirement in 1973 and reclaimed his Rebels from Billy Kinard. Billy had been appointed head coach in 1971 by his brother, Bruiser Kinard, who had taken over as athletic director when Coach Vaught was taken ill. The Bruiser was another of Mississippi's living legends. He had been an All-American at Ole Miss and All-Pro with the Green Bay Packers. With Bruiser and Billy back on the sidelines, Coach Vaught completely reshuffled the 1973 Rebels and marched them up to Knoxville, where they upset Johnny Majors and the Vols, 21–0. "Ol' Johnny, he had us scouted pretty good. He was sure he was gonna stop us cold. So I juggled our lineup, and by the time Johnny figured out who was playin' where, the game was over."

The chairman called the committee to order, and after quickly plowing through its routine business affairs, he asked Avery to introduce his guest. Avery's introduction was lengthy and inflated. According to Avery, I had been all over the United States, carrying the entire conservation movement on my broad shoulders. After looking at the whole country, I had settled on Mississippi as America's best hope for protecting its great natural heritage. "This here Dave Morine has seen it all," Avery concluded. "He comes from Boston, and he's been to all of them fancy schools up there. Believe me, this boy, he knows what he's talkin' about."

Avery sat down and started puffing nervously. Everyone was puffing. The room was blue with smoke. My eyes were watering; I could hardly see through the haze. I got up, told the committee how honored I was to be in the great state of Mississippi, and began my plea. "Mississippi is unique because she still has a chance to determine her own destiny. Growth is going to come to Mississippi. She is still rich in natural and human resources, and industry needs those resources. Mississippi is like a pure young woman. Her virtue must be protected. She should be looking for a lasting relationship with industry, one in which she remains an equal partner. She must preserve her dowry of natural resources, rather than allow industry to plunder it." I paused. I could see Avery's eyes flicking nervously around the room. Maybe I was spreading it on too thick with my pure-young-woman analogy, but it was too late to change now. "If Mississippi allows herself to be raped by out-of-state industry, she has no one to blame but herself."

There was a brief silence while the members mulled over what I had just said. Coach Vaught was the first to speak. "This boy's made a good point. We've got it pretty good down here. We shouldn't just give the ball to those big bidness boys from out of state." He looked at Avery. Everyone looked at Avery. "What play you callin', Avery?"

"Coach, we gotta put some points on the board. Right now we're way behind. We own only 20,000 acres for game management. Tennessee's got close to 200,000; Louisiana's got over 250,000; Florida's got 120,000; hail, even Alabama's got 40,000." At the mention of Alabama, people straightened up and puffed even harder. Avery knew how to motivate his team. "Dave, why don't you tell the committee about the Pascagoula?"

The week before, Avery and I had gone down to Pascagoula and toured the swamp. It really was an amazing place. The Pascagoula Hardwood Company owned 42,000 acres of virgin land. It encompassed forty-five miles of the Pascagoula River, more than fifty natural ox-bow lakes, and ten miles of frontage along Black Creek, the state's most popular canoeing stream. There were Indian mounds and thousand-year-old cypress trees, some of them as much as thirty feet in circumference. "If Mississippi is really serious about preserving her natural heritage," I concluded, "it is doubtful that she will ever have another opportunity to acquire such an incredibly large, beautiful, and ecologically significant tract of land." I sat down.

The questioning began. The discussion lasted for two hours; it was the toughest grilling I had ever been through. It was worse than an IRS audit. These guys were not naturalists. All they wanted to know was how the purchase of the Pascagoula lands would enhance the profitability of the state's game and fish business.

They wanted to know how much timber was on the property. How many sportsman user-days could it accommodate? What was the population within one hour's drive. Two hours' drive? Three hours' drive? How many users would be out-of-staters? What was the price of a nonresident license, and how much could they increase it? How much hunting could the property support? Who hunted it now? Were there any on-site studies of fishing in the Pascagoula River Basin?" And on, and on, and on.

Finally, the chairman moved that the committee request $15 million from the legislature for the purchase of the Pascagoula Hardwood Company's lands. The motion was seconded by Coach Vaught. It passed unanimously. The committee adjourned.

Avery was euphoric. I was drained. "How'd I do?" I asked, fishing for a compliment.

"Hail, you were talkin' so fast, they only got about half of what you said, but that was enough. Now it's time to get to work." Avery said it as if we hadn't done a thing so far. "I've got to push this bill through the legislature, and you've got to go get that land."

Avery spent most of the next three months over at the legislature, lobbying. I spent my time in New York, Washington, and Laurel, meeting with various members of the four families. My friend had been right; the younger generation wanted to sell. What he had neglected to tell me was that the younger generation had very little control over the company. The biggest block of stock, close to 25 percent, was controlled by a distinguished old gentleman in Laurel. The patriarch of one of the four families, he was perfectly content to leave things just the way they were. He felt that this land was a good investment. He had no desire to sell. "We've held these lands for close to half a century," he told me on one occasion. "Back when we got 'em, this swamp was worth nothing'. If we sold 'em, we'd end up givin' half their value away in taxes. Mr. Morine, they's nothin' I hate more than payin' taxes."

The fact that the lands would be sold for conservation purposes appealed to many members of the other families, and the younger generation wanted the money, but it was clear that nobody was willing to try an end run around the old patriarch. I elected not to pass this information on to Avery. Why upset him when he was so busy trying to get the money, especially when the funding still looked like a long shot? Better for Avery to fail than me.

At 2:00 A.M. on March 20, 1975, I was jarred awake by the phone. When I picked up the receiver, it was Avery. His first words were, "Bubba, we done pulled this caper off!"

He was sitting in the governor's office. He described how, in one of the most dramatic sessions in the history of the legislature, they had approved $15 million for the purchase of the Pascagoula Hardwood lands. Avery wanted me at the next meeting of the Wildlife Heritage Committee. It was time to present the project.

The governor was planning to sign the bill at a public ceremony early the following week. The committee would meet right after the signing. "You just tell 'em how to sign the check an' we're on our way." Avery could hardly contain himself. He was ecstatic when he hung up. I was petrified. I had exactly five days to figure out what to do.

I was sitting in Pat Noonan's office when he came in the next morning. I had tossed and turned all night, searching for a solution. I had come up with squat. "Pat. What am I going to do?" I pleaded. "Those guys are going to kill me."

"Dave," he exclaimed incredulously, "you call this a problem? If we can't figure out how to spend $15 million in Mississippi, we're in the wrong business. Get down there and sell them on another project. You're telling me there's only one swamp in all of Mississippi?"

Another project, of course. Why hadn't I thought of that? There were thirty million acres in Mississippi. With $15 million in our pockets, how hard could it be to find another project?

The committee members were aglow when I entered the conference room. They were all rehashing the governor's signing ceremony. It had been a huge success. Avery had engineered press coverage by all of the major papers in the Southeast. Nobody could believe that Mississippi, the poorest state in the union, had appropriated $15 million for conservation. The chairman immediately waived the reading of the minutes and turned the meeting over to me. "Now that we've got the money, Dave, let's hear about the deal." Everybody settled back to enjoy their cigars and the fruits of their hard-earned victory.

"Mississippi is a state blessed with a great natural heritage," I began. There was much smiling and nodding. "It is a state with many significant natural areas. What Mississippi needs now is a comprehensive natural heritage program that will identify all of these areas and set mechanisms in place for protecting them."

"Dave," said the chairman, "that's all well and good, and we sure are interested in protectin' our great natural heritage, but what about the Pascagoula?"

"Well, the Pascagoula's a good project, but it's not the only project we should be considering. Now that the legislature has given you $15 million, it would be foolish to put all our eggs in one basket. We should look at a number of projects across the state."

There was some serious puffing and mumbling. I looked at the coach.

"With all this money, you need to devise a total game plan. The Pascagoula is just one play. And, as I'm sure Coach Vaught will agree, you can't go for the touchdown on every play."

Now there was stone silence. The committee realized that I was shifting gears, that after all my hype about the Pascagoula, I couldn't deliver.

The coach stroked his granite chin. His presence filled the room. "Son," he said in his soft, deep drawl, "down here we go for the touchdown on every play. Now you march on back to Laurel and git us that property." That was the end of the shortest meeting in the history of the Wildlife Heritage Committee. The members filed out.

Avery sat there in shock. "Bubba, what the hail you doin'?"

"Avery," I confessed, "the Pascagoula property is not for sale."

"Not for sale? The hail it ain't. I got $15 million that says it is. I got the money, now you get the property. That's the deal."

Avery was right. If we couldn't buy the Pascagoula property, the Conservancy was dead in Mississippi, and probably the entire Southeast. We had to go for the touchdown.

After I got home, I sat in my office for two days, wracking my brain, trying to find a solution. The owners had us scouted. They knew our playbook. What would the coach do? He'd juggle the lineup.

I called Avery. "Avery," I said, "if we can't buy the land, let's buy the corporation."

"Bubba," he said, "now you're talkin'."

Working with the best legal and financial minds we could find, the Conservancy devised a totally new play. The Conservancy would make a tender offer for 75 percent of the company's stock, implement a tax-free dissolution of the corporation, trade the patriarch 25 percent of the land for his family's stock, and sell the remaining 75 percent of the land to the state. We would use the state's appropriation to pay back the money we had borrowed to buy the stock.

The patriarch approved the plan. It got him his land, tax-free, and got the younger generation out of his hair. The younger generation and the remaining stockholders were very pleased. Not only had they done something good for the state of Mississippi, they had turned a previously dead asset into some real money. Avery and the Wildlife Heritage Committee were jubilant. They had acquired the finest state wildlife management area in the Southeast, laid the foundation for the best wildlife heritage program in America, and best of all, gained some serious yardage on Alabama. The Conservancy was equally pleased. Not only had we helped save a major bottomland hardwood forest, but now we could hold up Mississippi's Wildlife Heritage Program as a challenge to other states. This was the decoy that Pat needed to lure more sportsmen's dollars into the Conservancy.

As for me, I was glad to get out of Mississippi in one piece. Thanks to a kick in the butt from Coach Vaught, I had juggled the lineup and gone for the score. As Avery put it during his remarks at the dedication of the Pascagoula Wildlife Management Area, "Ol' Dave here, he done had us scared for a while, but for a fast-talkin' Yankee, he done all right. He done scored the touchdown."

Professional Courtesy

THE NATURE CONSERVANCY is often described as the most businesslike of the nonprofit conservation organizations. Articles about the Conservancy inevitably point out that it is run by lawyers and MBAs, how it wheels and deals, how it focuses on the "bottom line." This description is true. The Conservancy's MBAs are constantly developing strategies, crunching numbers, and hammering out deals, while its lawyers trudge through legal descriptions, study statutes, and agonize over affidavits.

What these articles fail to mention is that the Conservancy's lawyers and MBAs are usually not very good naturalists; that they tend to become babes once they enter the woods. One of the Conservancy's cardinal rules is that we do not mix nature with business.

I am one of the Conservancy's MBAs. While I greatly appreciate our natural world, my knowledge of it is extremely limited. It is a waste of time for me to evaluate the natural attributes of a piece of land. We have botanists and biologists who are far better qualified than I am to determine the ecological significance of a potential preserve.

But they get out of the way when it comes time to make the deal. Mutual respect and professional courtesy dictate that our lawyers and MBAs spend their time communing with money and leave nature to the naturalists.

Nonetheless, every now and then a Conservancy lawyer or MBA is forced to meet nature head-on. The result is usually disastrous.

My worst experience came in the spring of 1976. I was working on a little project near Charlottesville, Virginia. This preserve is not one of the Conservancy's more spectacular natural areas. It's a hundred acres of second-growth woods and floodplain that protect the watershed of a small creek. I became involved because a very generous donor had committed a substantial amount of money for the acquisition of this area. This donor insisted that I personally inspect the property and handle all negotiations.

A key tract we hoped to protect was called Hidden Springs. It was a country estate with nearly a mile of frontage on the creek, and it controlled the upper slopes of the watershed. If it were developed, the resulting siltation and septic runoff would inevitably degrade the natural qualities of our preserve. Hidden Springs was owned by a professor emeritus at the university and his wife.

Unfortunately, the Professor and his wife, Louise, were not members of the Conservancy. Our research showed that they were well-off, childless, and totally committed to the University of Virginia. I was sure that Hidden Springs was destined to be willed to the university. If that happened, the area would be in serious jeopardy. In my opinion, schools, churches, and other nonprofits are among the most callous landowners in the country; to them, land is purely a commodity from which they have a fiduciary duty to squeeze every last nickel. Judging from what had happened to the rest of Charlottesville, the university seemed to have little concern for the preservation of open space.

They'd probably have bulldozers grinding over Hidden Springs while the overseers were still chipping the Professor's name onto the Rotunda.

I called the Professor and Louise to set up a meeting. They were most cordial. They had met our generous donor and claimed to be very sympathetic to the Conservancy's objectives. They insisted that I come for dinner. They even implied that I was welcome to spend the night.

My strategy was simple. I was going to ask them to donate a conservation easement over Hidden Springs. A conservation easement seemed like the perfect solution. The Professor and Louise could own Hidden Springs for the rest of their lives, and upon their demise they could leave it to the university, but the property could never be developed without the Conservancy's approval. The Professor and his wife would get a substantial tax write-off, the university could still make a bundle by selling the property as a country estate, and our preserve would be protected in perpetuity. All I had to do was sell the deal to the Professor and Louise.

The evening couldn't have started any better. It was cool and clear, with the scent of new grass and wildflowers wafting from the fields. The Professor, bedecked in a UVA tie and a blue blazer with a Cavalier embroidered on its breast pocket, poured three bourbon and branches into silver UVA cups. He and Louise escorted me to the patio. In the twilight, I could see the creek below, and beyond it, the Rotunda, the centerpiece of Mr. Jefferson's university. "Ah," I said, sipping my bourbon, "it's a pleasure to be back in Charlottesville. I received a fine education here, at the Business School."

They looked at each other and nodded approvingly.

Louise and the Professor were a calm, gracious, dignified couple. The Professor still taught a course on Faulkner. He was surprised when I confessed that I had forgotten "The Bear." He immediately produced a dog-eared copy. "I'm sure that as a conservationist you'll recognize this passage," he said. "Let me refresh your memory." The cool of the evening crept over Hidden Springs, and Louise suggested that we move inside by the fire.

Out of nowhere, an elderly butler in a heavily starched white serving jacket appeared with a bucket of ice, a bottle of Virginia Gentleman, and a silver UVA pitcher filled with good Virginia branch. He recharged our cups as the Professor settled into his UVA captain's chair and began to read aloud.

Then I remembered why I had forgotten "The Bear." The Professor went on, and on, and on. He didn't finish with Faulkner until we were ready to be seated for dinner. As we walked into the dining room, a full moon could be seen rising through the windows. A Black Angus was lowing at the Milky Way. The three of us took our places at the table as long as one of Faulkner's sentences. Another fire was ablaze, and I watched the flames flicker in my crystal wine glass as the Professor intoned grace. Once the meal had been properly blessed, Louise tinkled a little bell. Out came the soup, and I prepared myself to strike.

It is accepted practice within the Conservancy that you always make your pitch just before the soup. The setup was perfect. I took another sip of wine. My palate was tingling with the taste of success. The deal was as good as done.

I was clearing my throat to speak when a cry came from the kitchen. "Professor! Professor! Come quick, we done got ourselves a snake!" Snake? My mouth suddenly went dry as dust.

The Professor looked over apologetically. "Please excuse me. Missy seems to be upset about something." He got up from the table and purposefully strode off into the kitchen.

I smiled at Louise. She smiled back. "It's probably nothing. Missy gets excited over the least little thing. I'm sure my husband can handle it."

I hoped so. I soon heard the Professor stomping up the cellar stairs. "Sakes alive! You should see the size of that snake! He must be six feet if he's an inch. I don't believe I've ever seen one quite that big." He stood in the doorway to the dining room with his arms outstretched.

I had read somewhere that the length of a person's outstretched arms equaled his height, which, coincidentally, was roughly the length of a fathom. All I could fathom from this scene was that there was one big snake downstairs. Louise and the Professor looked at me. The message was clear. They didn't have to say it: What luck! We have the biggest snake we've ever seen, right in our own cellar, and here's a professional conservationist to remove it!

I felt obliged to say something. "This is really an *excellent* wine." I poured myself another glass as I tried to figure out what to do. "Don't worry about the snake," I said as nonchalantly as I could. "It's probably just come in to get out of the cold. If we leave it alone, I'm sure it will find its way out."

Louise looked at me incredulously. "Leave it alone? We most certainly will not leave it alone. This is my house, and I shall not have a snake upsetting my help. That snake is going out, and it's going out now." With that, she got up and marched toward the cellar. The Professor followed directly.

I had no choice. I fell in behind the Professor. As we passed through the kitchen, I saw Missy and the butler huddled in a corner, their eyes wide with fear. Louise hesitated at the top of the stairs. The Professor manfully assumed the lead. When we reached the bottom step, I could see a light coming from an open door. It was a cellar pantry. We tiptoed toward the light and peeked into the pantry.

The Professor pointed to a shelf in the far corner. "There he is," he whispered. "Do you see him?"

I looked at the shelf. I didn't see any snake. Then I rocked back in abject terror as the whole shelf readjusted itself. There was a rattle of glass. The snake was laced around an entire row of preserves. It seemed to be everywhere. My eyes widened as they followed its long black body around and around until they finally reached its head. The snake was staring directly at me. It cocked its head menacingly, its red tongue flitting in and out. I seriously thought I was going to wet my pants. What was a snake doing in the pantry? I prayed that it would slither away. It didn't. It just lay there, as if to say, "Okay, Mr. MBA. Come move me."

Louise broke the silence. "Goodness gracious! It *is* the biggest snake I've ever seen!" She turned to me. "Be careful it doesn't bite you!"

I fought to keep my composure. I tried to chuckle, but my voice cracked. "It's, ahem, just a black snake. You're lucky to have him. You won't have any mice or rats with this fellow around, ha, ha. I suggest we just ignore him. He'll leave when he's ready."

Louise was firm. "He'll leave right now!" She turned to the Professor. "Isn't that right, dear."

The Professor was equally firm. "Yes, by all means! It can't stay here. It's upsetting the help."

I knew that if I could walk into that room, grab that snake, and throw it outside, Hidden Springs and our new preserve would be protected in perpetuity. If real conservationists were throwing themselves in front of bulldozers and standing in front of harpoon guns, surely the least I could do was pick up a snake. I took a step. The snake hissed menacingly. I recoiled. I felt a warm trickle down the inside of my thigh. There was no way I was going to walk into that room and grab that snake. They didn't teach snake-grabbing at the Business School.

I tried one last orderly retreat. "Black snakes aren't poisonous, but one that size can give you a nasty bite. If you're determined to move him, which I don't recommend, I suggest we find something to grab it."

"The tongs!" exclaimed the Professor. "I'll get the tongs from the fireplace. They should do the trick."

"Good idea," I said. "I'll help you."

"No, no. You stay here and keep an eye on that fellow. We don't want him slipping away."

Louise stood there silently as the Professor bounded up the stairs. The snake didn't move. The only thing slipping away was my deal. The Professor was back in a flash. He was in good shape for a man his age. UVA might have to wait a while before it got its hands on Hidden Springs. That was fortunate. The Conservancy would need all the time it could get to resell the Professor and Louise on the idea of a conservation easement. My credibility was just about shot.

The Professor proferred the tongs, but I was too quick for him. "I'll get the cellar door," I said, looking back over my shoulder. "Try to grab him right behind the head." I opened the door with a flourish. "Okay. Any time you're ready."

The Professor entered the pantry. He was a brave man, but then again, it was his house. Louise backed away to the foot of the stairs. I could hear the Professor snapping away with the tongs. "Dammit, hold still, you rascal!" A jar shattered as it hit the floor. "Aha, there, now I've got you!" Louise started to run up the stairs as the Professor burst from the pantry. In front of him was the snake, twisting and twirling. I could see its white belly. He must have grabbed it somewhere in the middle, because both ends were thrashing wildly.

I tensed as they came hurtling toward me. Suddenly the Professor let out a shriek. One end of the snake had wrapped itself around his hand. He dropped the tongs. The snake fell to the floor. It swayed back and forth, trying to get its bearings. It sensed its escape and came wriggling right at me. I stumbled in panic out the cellar door and ran smack into a wall. The impact knocked me off my feet. I started groping my way up the stone steps. I froze as I felt all six feet of the snake slither over me and disappear into the darkness.

I got up. I tried to dust myself off, but my hands wouldn't stop shaking. Slowly, I followed the light back into the cellar. The Professor had picked up the tongs and was going up the stairs with Louise. I took a deep breath, straightened my tie, and sheepishly followed. I heard the Professor reassuring Missy and the butler as he passed through the kitchen. "No need to worry now. That old snake is back outside where it belongs."

"Thank goodness. We don't need no snakes around here," Missy said with great relief.

"You're absolutely right, Missy, but it's all over now. Let's clean up that broken jar and finish our meal."

I went back to the table and dutifully delivered my pitch. I should have just gone home. The snake had ruined everything. Louise and the Professor were polite but cool. They kept looking at me as if they had just caught me cheating on an exam. I could no longer be trusted. Anybody who was afraid to pick up a snake couldn't be much of a conservationist. I wasn't quite through with my pecan pie when Louise pointedly reminded me that it was a long drive back to Washington.

To this date, we have no conservation easement over Hidden Springs and no guarantee that the creek will be protected in perpetuity.

Every now and then I think of the Professor and Louise and what might have been if I had walked into that room, picked up that snake, and thrown it outside. And then I think of the snake. Why wasn't it down by the creek where it belonged? I was in a house, where I belonged, with silver cups and fine china, communing with money. It was the snake that was wrong. It had broken one of the Conservancy's cardinal rules; it had mixed nature with business. It should have shown some respect and excused itself when it saw that it was blowing my deal. Whatever happened to professional courtesy?

The Price of Gumption

THE NATIONAL PARK SERVICE is one of the most controversial land managers in America. The controversy stems from Congress's 1916 mandate that the Park Service administer the parks for the general public, ". . . for the enjoyment of same, in such manner and by such means as will leave them unimpaired for the enjoyment of future generations."

This paradox is not new. It was first set forth in Genesis 1:28, where God says to man, "Be fruitful and multiply, and replenish the earth and subdue it."

When God laid down his law, there were just Adam and Eve, and neither of them drove. When Congress laid down its law, there were still only 100 million Americans and fewer than 1 million cars. Today, there are 250 million Americans driving more than 200 million motor vehicles. We are the most mobile society in the world, and thanks to that mobility, our national parks are being overrun. Americans like to drive to their parks; when they get there, they like to motor right up to the sights, find a place to park, and visit the concession stands.

That's how most Americans would define enjoyment, and that's what they expect from the National Park Service.

Conservationists are appalled by this mentality. They define enjoyment as hiking through the wilderness and sleeping on the ground. They expect the National Park Service to keep the parks pristine natural areas. According to Edward Abbey, the late author and most vocal proponent of eco-terrorism, the Park Service has become divided into two camps: the "developers," those who see their job as providing enjoyment, and the "preservers," those who want to leave the parks unimpaired for future generations. Given this type of criticism, it is no wonder that the National Park Service is the focus of such controversy.

Even though I worked for The Nature Conservancy, I hadn't had much contact with the National Park Service until 1974. That's when we moved to Great Falls, Virginia. Our next-door neighbor happened to be the Great Falls National Park.

Another neighbor was Dick Saltonstall. Dick was an avid outdoorsman and environmental writer. He had just left *Time* and was working on his third book, *A Maine Pilgrimage,* when we met him. He soon became a close friend. Dick was a true conservationist. He recycled, composted, and made a conscious effort to conserve energy long before it was fashionable. When it came to the national parks, he was a dedicated preservationist. Dick's criticism of the Park Service was focused on one particular issue: its management of the Colorado River.

On January 1, 1977, my wife and I were invited to the Saltonstall's home for New Year's dinner. It was a cold rainy day. I didn't feel much like eating. We had bid farewell to 1976 by cleaning out Dick's wine cellar, and I was suffering the effects. I was hoping that a long walk in the Great Falls National Park would clear my head and restore my appetite. Dinner at the Saltonstalls' would be delicious. It always was.

I asked Dick if he wanted to come with me on my walk. That was a mistake. I should never have mentioned the park. My muddled mind had forgotten about Dick's battle with the National Park Service over the Colorado River. I had heard it all before. I had been hearing about it ever since I had known him. For three years, Dick had been urging me to get The Nature Conservancy involved.

"If I go for a walk, it'll be on my own land," he said indignantly. "I wouldn't give those simple-minded bureaucrats the satisfaction of using their park."

I nodded wearily. There was no stopping him now.

"How can those idiots think they can restrict private individuals like Joe Munroe from using the river?" Joe Munroe was a photographer who had been a stringer at *Time* with Dick. He was also a river rat who liked to run the Grand Canyon in wooden dories. Joe's trips weren't much different from that of Major John Wesley Powell, the one-armed Civil War veteran who had made the first recorded trip through the Canyon a hundred years earlier.

For the better part of those hundred years, the only people who had shot the Canyon did it, like Joe Munroe, in wooden dories. The advent of the rubber raft changed all that. Rubber rafts are ideal for running rivers with major rapids, like the Colorado. By 1972, the Grand Canyon was being overrun with rafters, and its fragile ecology could not stand this onslaught. The National Park Service had to do something.

What it did was adopt new regulations which, for all practical purposes, limited rafting permits to licensed professional outfitters. These regulations meant that private individuals like Joe Munroe and Dick Saltonstall found it almost impossible to obtain a permit.

Dick and Joe flipped out. What right did the National Park Service have to exclude private individuals from the Colorado River? Why were licensed professional outfitters, who Dick maintained exploited the river as much as any developer, given preferred status? None of them knew the Canyon better than Joe Munroe. Dick and Joe were determined to overturn this regulation. They founded something called the "Wilderness Public Rights Fund," and in 1972 they sued the Federal government.

"Dick," I said for what must have been the hundredth time, "why do you keep batting your head against the wall? You can't take on the National Park Service and expect to get anywhere."

"Nonsense, me boy," he responded. "All it takes is a little gumption."

Dick was loaded with gumption. His case had been dragging on for over four years. His oldest son was almost big enough to run the Grand Canyon, but Dick made it clear that no son of his would ever run the Colorado with a professional outfitter. If he went at all, he was going with Joe Munroe.

My head was killing me. "Dick, let me go for my walk while it's still light," I said, hoping to escape. "We can discuss your lawsuit over dinner."

The sky was dark with intermittent showers. I decided to drive to the falls, even though they are only a mile from my house. That way, I could retreat to the car if the rain got too heavy. I'm not much of an outdoorsman. I like my own environment warm and dry.

Not surprisingly, the parking lot was almost empty. I decided to walk the trail that runs right along the Potomac. Usually the trail around the falls is loaded with tourists. Today I enjoyed having it all to myself. I stopped at each of the overlooks. The river was high and steel-gray. A couple of kayakers were balanced on a big wave that formed just below the falls. I pushed on. I could feel a sweat starting to break under my windbreaker. My head began to clear. I loved walking in the park, especially when there was no one there. I thought about Dick's lawsuit. I had no problems with the National Park Service. I liked the way they managed the parks.

As I jogged back to the car, I reflected on how fortunate I was to live next to both Dick and the park. I had two wonderful neighbors. How many people could spend the afternoon enjoying the beauty of a national park, and then walk next door for a gourmet meal with a great conservationist? Tonight, I'd do myself a favor and not mention the Park Service.

My mood was broken when I got back to the car. There was a ticket on my windshield. This had to be a mistake. I was in a legal parking space. In fact, I was the only car in the lot. I pulled the ticket out from under my wiper. It was not a mistake. It was a citation from the National Park Service, dated 1/1/77, 4:17 P.M. The offense: Expired Tag. The fine: $50.00.

I flipped out. My tags weren't expired. I just didn't have a '77 sticker on my rear license plate. I had tried to put it on that morning, but changing your stickers is one of those little tasks you should never undertake hung over. I'd stuck the rear sticker on upside down. When I tried to take it off, it had ripped. Then the pieces wouldn't re-stick. I finally ended up taping the pieces to my registration. That was the best I could do. If a cop stopped me, I could prove that my car was properly registered.

I'd had my wife mount the sticker on the front. She'd done it perfectly. Whoever had given me the ticket obviously hadn't checked the front plate. I hate laziness, especially when it's going to cost me fifty bucks.

I jumped in the car and drove over to the Information Center. I told the ranger on duty that there had been a mistake. I showed him my registration with the sticker taped to it. The ranger, a sincere-looking young man wearing a Smokey the Bear hat, maintained that he had nothing to do with tickets. Tickets came under the jurisdiction of the park police.

I was becoming more enraged by the minute. "Where can I find these park police?"

"Nowhere," replied the young ranger. "They just drive around the park. They don't have an office."

My head began to throb. The ranger could see that I was about to explode. "There is one number we could try," he added nervously. He dialed the number. He looked at me encouragingly. "I've got 'em," he whispered.

The young ranger started to explain my problem. I didn't like what I heard. He kept saying things like, "Oh, I see. Of course. Absolutely right."

I reached over and grabbed the phone. I tried my best to be polite. "Pardon me, are you the officer who just gave me a ticket?"

A voice on the other end said, "Most likely, since I'm the only officer on duty."

I started to explain his mistake. He interrupted me. "If you disagree with the charge, check Box B and mail it to the address indicated on the ticket within ten days."

I looked at the ticket. Box B indicated that I wanted a hearing before a U.S. Magistrate. That meant I would have to go to court. The small print said that I would be liable for an additional $25.00 in court fees if I were found guilty. Now I was really steamed.

I took a deep breath. "If I check Box B, I'll have to go to court."

"That's correct." the voice on the other end of the line agreed.

"I have a better idea," I said through clenched teeth. "Since I'm here, you're here, the car's here, my registration's here, and the ripped tag's here, why don't we just get together and settle this matter? That way I won't have to take a morning off, and the taxpayers won't have to pay for a court appearance."

"Sir, if you have a problem with the ticket, check Box B and mail it to the address indicated on the ticket within ten days." I might as well have been talking to a recording.

I lost it. "Why don't you take Box B and shove it!" I screamed into the phone. The line went dead.

I was still burning when I got to Dick's house. "Now I have to pay fifty bucks because some cop was too lazy to get out of his car and check both plates. I thought the park was supposed to be for my enjoyment. You'd think the Park Service had better things to do than spend their time checking car tags? What does the National Park Service care about tags? What do they have to do with running a park? The government's just trying to fleece the public. And where does the money go?"

"Not to the parks, I can assure you of that," Dick said, egging me on. "That money goes right into the general fund. Your fifty bucks is going to help pay for another bureaucrat."

"The hell it is!" I said. "Where's that damn ticket?" Dick had been looking at it. He gave it back to me. "Gimme your pen." Dick quickly produced a pen. I took the pen and firmly checked Box B. "I'm going to court!"

Dick hoisted his glass. "Now, there's some gumption! I'll drive you!"

I didn't hear from the government for over three months. I assumed that they had forgotten me, that the officer had come to his senses and squashed the ticket. Then on March 10, I received a notice from the U.S. Magistrate captioned *United States of America vs. Morine, David.* I was scheduled to appear before the Magistrate at the U.S. District Court, Essex Building, 33 North Fairfax Street, Alexandria, Virginia, on April 2 at 10:00 A.M. to answer the charge: Exp Tag.

I brought the notice over to Dick. He studied it with great interest. "Davey, me boy, I'm proud of you. You've taken a stand. We'll use this case to determine why the National Park Service has chosen to involve itself in state and local matters, and more than that, why they don't put the proceeds back into the parks. It's a two-pronged test."

I began to have second thoughts. I wasn't sure I wanted to challenge the sovereignty of the federal government. "Gee, Dick, I don't know," I wavered. "All I want to do is get out of paying the ticket."

"Nonsense, me boy!" he said with great conviction. "We've got a sure-fire case here. Ironclad. This is their Achilles heel. If we can get a ruling that prohibits the park police from citing for state violations, we can parlay that into a writ of mandamus for failure of jurisdiction." He stroked his chin. "We might even get a petition for certiorari to the appellate level."

Dick sounded like a jackleg lawyer. My case was getting out of hand. "Look, Dick," I said, "why don't I just go down, show them my tags, and get this thing dismissed? Let's not make a federal case out of it. Ha. Ha."

He didn't hear me. "Now's the time. Strike while the iron's hot. This is the case we've been looking for. At last, a chink in the armor, a jurisdictional issue. That's the ticket. Gumption, me boy. All it takes is gumption."

Dick was sitting in front of my house at 9:00 A.M. on April 2. He was driving his black '69 Volvo. This was Dick's city car. It looked very official. He had plastered a gold and black seal the size of a basketball on each side. The seal displayed the same eagle that was on the back of a quarter. The lettering at the top said, "United States of America, E Pluribus Unum." On the bottom, instead of "Quarter Dollar," were the words, "Official U.S. Taxpayer." Dick loved this insignia. He'd found it in some novelty shop when he was working for *Time.* He claimed it rendered the Volvo immune from tickets.

Dick was clearly excited as we made our way to Alexandria. He was carefully explaining the different points that he wanted me to challenge. "States' rights. Allocation of federal funds. Purpose of the National Park Service. Preservation versus development in the parks. Issuance of permits."

"Please, Dick," I pleaded, "I just want to get my ticket dismissed."

He didn't hear me. "Substantive due process. Procedural due process. Unconstitutionally vague . . ." And on, and on, and on.

We arrived at the Essex Building at 9:30. There were no parking spaces for the general public. The only open spots were in front of the courthouse. They were "Reserved for Government Vehicles Only." Dick pulled right in.

"You can't park here, Dick," I said. "Look at the signs."

"Official U.S. Taxpayer," he said, patting his door. He jumped out and bounded up the courthouse steps three at a time. I followed at a more sober pace. We asked the guard where to go. He pointed us to a room. We walked in and took our seats on a bench with a row of other defendants. They were a sullen group, mostly young males, all scruffy, some with tattoos. Dick's curly hair, rosy cheeks, and patrician good looks were totally out of place. It was as if Prince Charles had ventured into the cheap seats at Wembley.

At 9:40, a young man who identified himself as a Deputy Magistrate called for our attention. He was a tough little Italian with a clipboard. Were it not for his suit and tie, he could have been a coach checking his lineup before the game. He was, in fact, preparing the lineup for the day. It was his job to figure out who was there, what cases needed to be heard, and in what order. Dick, always the journalist, moved right behind him. He peered over the Deputy Magistrate's shoulder. At six-two, Dick was at least eight inches taller than the Deputy Magistrate. When the Deputy Magistrate called out a name, Dick would look at me and mouth the alleged offense.

"Alvarez!" the Deputy Magistrate shouted.

("Possession," mouthed Dick.)

"Columbo!"

("Auto theft.")

"Farber!"

("Mail fraud.")

"McLaughlin!"

("Extortion.")

"Morine!"

"Not guilty!" Dick said in a loud voice. The Deputy Magistrate turned around and gave Dick a studied look. "You Morine?" he asked.

"No. That's him," Dick replied, pointing to me.

The Deputy Magistrate took no notice of me. "Then who are you?"

"I'm a reporter covering the Morine case," Dick said with much bravado.

"A what!"

"A reporter," Dick repeated, more meekly. "I'm interested in the Morine case."

The Deputy Magistrate consulted his clipboard. "You're interested in an expired tag? Who the hell do you work for?"

Dick started to say something about freelancing. I quickly interrupted. "There seems to be some mistake," I said, very politely. "I had the tag, but it fell off. See? Here it is." I presented my registration with the ripped tag taped to it. "And," I continued, "here's a Polaroid of my car taken on January 1st that shows the sticker on the front plate. The officer just didn't bother to look." I pointed to the picture.

The Deputy Magistrate looked at my picture, scanned my registration, and said, "Okay. Case dismissed." Whereupon he scratched my name from the lineup.

"Wait a minute," said Dick. "We're not getting off that easy. We demand to see the judge."

The Deputy Magistrate looked confused. "I just dismissed the case. Why do you want to see the judge? You want to interview him about an expired tag?"

"That's not the issue." Dick said. "Morine wants to know under what authority the National Park Service checks state tags, and how it uses the money it collects from this illegal activity."

A combative look came across the face of the Deputy Magistrate. "Oh. Let me get this straight. You want to challenge the authority of the federal government."

"That's right!" Dick affirmed quite proudly.

The Deputy Magistrate took a hard look at me. "I'll be happy to put your name back on the docket, Mr. Morine, but I hope you got a lotta time and a lotta money if you expect to fight the federal government."

"Ah. Er. Ah," I stammered. "Well, on second thought, let's just forget the whole thing." Dick looked at me in disbelief, as if I had just thrown away the perfect case. I turned and walked out, not wanting to face him. He caught up with me on the steps. "Davey, me boy, where's your gumption?"

"Dick," I replied sheepishly, "gumption costs time and money. You're willing to pay the price. I'm not. You heard the guy. I can't take on the federal government."

Dick seemed to understand. He never again mentioned my lack of gumption. His own suit finally ran aground on the steps of the Supreme

Court when the justices refused to hear his case. But he didn't lose. During the course of appeals, the National Park Service revised its regulations so that 60 percent of the permits to run the Grand Canyon went to professional outfitters and 40 percent were reserved for individuals. He and Joe Munroe were waiting for their permit when Dick died suddenly in March of 1982. In the spring of 1984 his oldest son ran the Grand Canyon with Joe Munroe.

Bagging the Limit

MY FIRST INVITATION TO GO DUCK HUNTING came in the fall of 1978. It wasn't just any invitation. I was asked to hunt at the oldest, and arguably the most prestigious, hunt club in North America.

The Club was in Canada but was controlled by a group of Americans, all of whom had been born into the Social Register. Yet despite the members' uniformly deep pockets, operating expenses had become a burden for the Club. After much thought, the members came up with the idea of giving all of the Club's high ground to the Canadian government as a new national wildlife refuge. This disposition would cut their operating costs, and, hopefully, give them a whopping tax deduction.

That's when I received a call from the Minister of Natural Resources of Canada. He explained the problem. The Canadian government wanted to acquire the Club's land as a gift for a new national wildlife refuge, but the Americans would not make the donation unless they could be assured that the gift would qualify for a U.S. tax deduction and that the land would in fact be managed in perpetuity as a refuge.

"We've been eyeing this tract for years," the minister told me. "It's one of the premier natural areas in all of Canada. We'll do anything we can to get it, but these damn tax laws are a real bugger. Would you chaps mind having a go at it?"

I had been director of land acquisition for six years. During that time, we had done some innovative deals, and one of our lawyers, Mike Wright, was becoming an expert on using the U.S. tax code internationally. I thought that we might be able to figure something out. I knew that we wanted to meet the members of the oldest hunt club in North America, any one of whom could become a major supporter of the Conservancy. "We'd be happy to have a go at it," I told the minister.

The next week I flew to New York to have lunch with the president of the hunt club. In real life, he was the president and CEO of one of New York's major banks. We met in the president's private dining room. He was very affable; we got along right from the start.

I listened carefully as he outlined the situation. As I expected, the deal hinged on our being able to answer two questions. First, how could the Club donate the land so that the individual members would get a tax deduction, and second, how could the Club be sure that the Canadian government would be obligated to manage the land as a national wildlife refuge? Thanks to a plan devised by Mike Wright, I had answers to both of these questions.

Most of the old hunt clubs are stock corporations. The robber barons who formed these clubs back in the 1800s did not like partnerships; they liked corporations, especially when they controlled the stock.

Fortunately for the robber barons, they didn't have to deal with the Internal Revenue Service of 1978. The IRS looked upon the Club as a separate corporation. Unlike a partnership, a corporation cannot pass tax benefits through to the individual shareholders. Thus, the members of the Club would not get a deduction if the Club gave the land away. The only way that the members could claim a deduction was to give some of their stock in the corporation to a qualified U.S. charity.

Our solution was that the individual members would donate to the Conservancy shares of stock in the Club equal in value to the appraised fair market value of the land that the Canadian government wanted for the refuge. After an appropriate holding period, the Conservancy would redeem its stock in the Club for the land. This gift-and-redemption would take care of the first problem.

After we had redeemed the stock, we could transfer the land to the Canadian government subject to restrictions that would require the Canadian government to manage the land as a national wildlife refuge. Mike Wright had dug out some IRS rulings which indicated that this transfer would be a separate transaction and would have no adverse impact on the value of the individual members' donations. That would take care of the second problem.

Mike Wright's plan was pure genius. I finished my presentation and smugly settled back into the rich leather chair.

I fully expected the president to jump up and gratefully pump my hand. Instead, he frowned. He had detected a flaw. The land that the Club wanted to give away represented the bulk of the Club's value. That would make The Nature Conservancy the majority stockholder of the oldest and most prestigious hunt club in North America. The flaw in the plan was The Nature Conservancy. Who was The Nature Conservancy?

"Surely you have another alternative?" he asked, hopefully.

"No," I said, fidgeting in my chair. "We see no other alternative. This is it."

"If we accept your plan, you'll control the Club. How do you propose we limit your control?"

"You can't," I confessed. "The members will have to give their stock with no strings attached. Otherwise, they can't claim a deduction."

"How long would you have to hold our stock?"

"A minimum of two years," I replied.

"Two years!" exclaimed the president. He stared at me as if I had just asked him for a big loan with no collateral.

I smiled weakly. "I'm afraid so. If the Club wants to do this deal, they'll just have to trust us. We're not a bunch of tree-huggers. We take a businesslike approach to conservation, and some of us actually enjoy hunting."

"Hmm. Hunting." He stroked his chin in contemplation. "That's a thought. Do you think that you could come up to the Club, meet the members, and explain your plan—and, of course, do a little shooting?" It wasn't a question. It was an order. I was being summoned before the loan committee.

"Well, maybe," I hedged. Legally and financially, our plan would pass muster. What the committee wanted to review was The Nature Conservancy's social acceptability.

"Fine," said the president. "We'll expect you this weekend."

We were in trouble. I had never shot anything in my life. I am not opposed to hunting. I had just never had the opportunity to hunt.

Back at the office, Mike Wright was aghast. "You mean to say that our deal depends on your ability to shoot some ducks? When did you ever shoot anything?"

Good point, Mike Wright. "Relax, Mike," I said with a certain bravado. "I've got Cabela's, Bean's, and the Orvis catalogs. Let's pick out some duds. I'll do just fine."

We spent the next hour poring over the catalogs. Cabela's stuff looked the most practical, but it was too common. I'd fit right in drinking with John Riggins, but definitely be out of place at the classiest hunt club in North America. Bean's was a step up when it came to boots, but the rest of the catalog was too preppy. True to L.L.'s philosophy, Bean's was following the market. It no longer catered to the hunter.

Orvis looked like just the ticket. I pictured myself arriving at the Club bedecked in Orvis's Moleskin Slacks, Shotshell Belt, mallard-colored Chamois Shirt, Thornproof Gamekeeper Jacket, Outback Chukka Shoes, toting a Battenkill Duffel.

Then we checked the prices. Even Cabela was out of our range. Attention K-Mart Shoppers!

"Now that you're gonna look like hell, what about a gun?" Mike Wright asked.

"Gun? Do you think I'll need a gun?"

Mike groaned. "How else do you propose to shoot a duck?"

"We'll have to borrow one," I reasoned. "Who do we know that has a gun?"

"Ray has a gun, and it might even be a shotgun," Mike said.

Ray was our director of stewardship. Unlike the rest of us, he actually went out into the field once in a while. Sure enough, he had an old 12-gauge Remington 870 Wingmaster. It was pretty beat-up, but that was all right. It might even give me some credibility.

My first view of the Club came as the launch weaved through acres upon acres of prime marsh. I had expected to see a grand old building with weathered shingles and massive stone chimneys, similar to the legendary clubs that once dominated the Carolina marshlands. Instead, we pulled up to a series of little cottages on stilts, connected by wooden walkways. They were almost hidden by the marsh grass, like some shanty town tucked away in a Louisiana bayou. Maybe my K-Mart wardrobe would be all right after all.

The president was waiting on the dock. He looked concerned. I surmised that our plan had encountered some opposition. "Welcome to Canada," he said, extending his hand.

"Thank you, it's nice to be here." His grip was firm as he pulled me onto the dock. The pilot passed up my $9.95 Naugahyde Overnighter with a look of contempt. The president studied it inquisitively. "Interesting bag," he commented. "I've never seen one quite like it."

"Thank you," I replied. "Could you please hand me my gun?" The pilot produced the Remington with the same look of contempt.

"Ah. Brought your own gun, I see," said the president.

"Yes," I said proudly. "The Wingmaster and I go back quite a way."

"Oh dear, a 12-gauge? I'm sorry, I should have told you. We only shoot 20s here. Club rules, you know. I'll lend you one of mine."

So much for Ray's Wingmaster. "I'd appreciate that. I should have thought to bring my 20."

"No problem," he said. "We'll leave the Wingmaster right here in the boathouse." I watched as he shoved it under a pile of old life jackets. "Be sure not to forget it," he added.

The president showed me to my cabin. Each member had his own cabin, and each cabin was named after some part of a duck. I was staying in Widgeon Wings. It belonged to a legendary Wall Street financier who was now too old to use it. Widgeon Wings would pass to his oldest son when he died, but, as the president told me, "He'll be damned if his son is going to use it while he's still alive."

The interior of Widgeon Wings looked like an advertisement for Ducks Unlimited. The lampshades, the rugs, the glasses, and even the ashtrays were all covered with images of ducks. Some were flying, some were swimming, some were landing, some were taking off. In the painting over the head, two were flying united.

We spent the afternoon walking some of the land that the Canadian government wanted for the refuge. The refuge would encompass most of a sixteen-mile-long peninsula that jutted out into Lake Ontario. It was easy to see why the government was so eager to acquire it. The peninsula provided the last resting place for migrating birds before they crossed the lake. It was totally wild and loaded with all types of birds and animals. During our walk, we jumped duck, geese, deer, fox, and even a moose.

I was exhilarated as I washed up for dinner. The crisp, clear Canadian air had heightened my senses. Now that I had seen the area, I knew that it had to be protected.

I rummaged through my Naugahyde Overnighter and cut the price tags off a pair of khakis, docksiders, a checked tattersall shirt, and a lime green 100-percent cotton sweater. It wasn't Orvis, but I felt sure that I could pass as one of the boys.

I was wrong. When I got to Pintails, the main lodge and dining hall, I politely tapped the mallard-head knocker. A middle-aged aristocrat opened the door. I couldn't believe it. He was wearing a cashmere blazer and club tie. I heard the conversation behind him fade to a murmur. "Oh, my," he said. "No one is allowed in Pintails after five without jacket and tie. Club rules, you know."

"I don't have a coat and tie," I confessed. "I thought I was going hunting."

The president quickly came to my rescue. "Not to worry," he said reassuringly. "We've got everything you need down at Greenhead." Things were not going well. I didn't have the bearing of a majority stockholder.

When I reentered Pintails in the nicest jacket and tie I had ever worn, the president wasted no time getting into the presentation. The mechanics of our plan withstood all of the members' legal and financial questions. The only unanswered question was the Conservancy's social acceptability. Their man talked a good game, but it remained to be seen whether he could shoot. They would find that out in the morning.

After a hearty breakfast of poached eggs, kippers, and fried tomatoes, we donned our hunting gear and assembled at the dock. That was where we would meet our punts. Long, flat-bottomed boats are commonly called punts, but at the oldest and most prestigious hunt club in North America, a punt was both the boat *and* the guide who poled it through the marshes. Each member was assigned a punt for life. Your punt became part of your family. Like it or not, you were stuck with him and he with you.

The punts were all attired in well-worn but handsomely tailored hand-me-downs from the members. They looked like British gamekeepers. Several were calmly sucking on briarwood pipes as they poled their punts up to the dock. I was getting more and more nervous. Not a word was spoken. Everyone knew exactly what he was doing except me. I turned to a portly industrialist from Cleveland who was seated next to me. "Say," I inquired, "how far do you lead them up here?"

His eyebrows rose. "I beg your pardon?"

"You know," I stumbled on. "How far do you lead them up here?" I swung my gun, a beautiful little Beretta, to illustrate my question.

"Oh, I see," he said, somewhat condescendingly. "I suspect that you lead them up here the same as you lead them down there. Wherever that may be."

The president came over. He wanted to introduce me to my punt, a very old and very distinguished gentleman named Percy. Percy had been the punt for Widgeon Wings all his adult life. He eventually would punt for my absent host's son, provided, of course, that Percy outlived my absent host. "Nice to meet you, Percy," I said.

"My pleasure, sir." Percy had a pronounced English accent. He looked like he wasn't averse to a little nip before breakfast. "What say we push off."

I gingerly settled into the front of the punt. The president handed me my gun. "Be sure to bag the limit," he admonished.

"Stoke up the oven," I replied confidently. "We'll be having duck for lunch." My optimism rose as Percy poled the punt to our assigned section of the marsh. Ducks were everywhere. They looked like softballs as they floated by. I was sure that I could hit them.

Percy became more and more garrulous as we glided along. At first, I assumed that he was just an old gentleman that liked to talk. Then I noticed the flask he kept in his waders. Percy was getting sloshed.

After a while, he stopped poling, got out, and pushed our punt into the high grass. He took out a pocket knife, cut some long reeds, and began to camouflage the punt. It was a clear, cold day, and a stiff breeze from the lake beat hard against my face. Percy's bare hands should have been frozen, but by now he was fortified with antifreeze.

Once satisfied with our cover, Percy flopped back into the punt and handed me a box of shells. "Here you go, lad," he mumbled. "Now get yourself ready. They should be coming in shortly."

As I loaded up, I was startled to hear a loud quacking right behind me. It was Percy. He sounded more like a duck than a duck did. Two curious greenheads immediately swooped in for a look. I was transfixed by their graceful motions as they set their wings and glided toward us, swaying back and forth into the wind. "Shoot, man, shoot!" Percy shouted.

I raised the Beretta, took aim, and pulled the trigger. Nothing happened. The ducks veered off and retreated over the marsh. "What the hell?" I exclaimed, studying the gun.

"The safety, lad, you must remove the safety."

Not to worry. Within a few minutes, four canvasbacks responded to Percy's calls. Bang. Bang. I squeezed off two shots. Nothing fell. Percy groaned. "Too low, lad. Block them out with your barrel. Reload, quick!" Bang. Bang. "Behind him! You're way behind him! Follow through, lad. You must follow through. Quick, reload!" Quack, quack. Bang, bang. Nothing. "Swing, man! Swing! Swing with the bird!" Bang, bang. Nothing. "By Jove, don't shoot at the lot of them! Pick one bird and stay on him!" Bang, bang. Nothing. Bang, bang. Quack, quack. Bang, bang. Nothing. The Beretta was steaming. I reached for more shells. The box was empty. "Percy, I need more shells."

Percy slipped the flask back into his waders, reached into his finely tailored jacket, and produced another box. "Here you go, lad, but mind you, this is it."

"What?"

"Two boxes is all you get. Club rules, you know."

"No sweat," I assured him. "I was just warming up. Get ready to jump into that marsh. They're going to be dropping like flies."

Fifteen shots later, I was still cold. "Percy," I said. "How many birds do I need to bag the limit?"

Percy thought for a minute. Clearly his flask was getting the better of him. "It depends on what you shoot, and when you shoot them. But ten birds is generally the limit." I could see that he thought it a foolish question. There was no way I was going to get ten birds. I'd be lucky to get one.

"Percy," I said. "You ever shoot one of these things?"

Percy smiled smugly. "Yes, sir. I've been known to take a duck."

"Do you think you can shoot my limit?"

Percy cocked his head proudly. "Your limit, sir, is in the bag."

I was taking a gamble. I knew that Percy was in the bag, but what choice did I have. "Remember," I cautioned, "we only have ten shells."

"That should be enough. Here, move to the rear, if you please." I thought for sure that Percy was going to tip us over as he wobbled to the front of the punt. Somehow we managed to exchange places.

A lone pintail was the first to test Percy. He dropped him cleanly. Next, a pair of widgeons came winging by. Percy took both with a couple of beautifully executed passing shots. I watched in amazement as a flock of blue-winged teal dropped in flawless formation in response to Percy's call. I could hardly follow them as they whooshed over our little blind. Percy raised and fired. Nothing. He scowled at the Beretta. "Bloody Eye-talians."

Two stragglers wheeled into the wind for another look. They were coming in low and fast. Percy lined them up and fired. They both dropped with one shot. Percy looked very pleased with himself. "There," he said, "that evens us up."

He then took a redhead, a pair of canvasbacks, and finished up with two drakes. He had bagged the limit.

The president was waiting for us at the dock. We were late. I could see that he was worried. I turned to Percy, who had, of course, reclaimed his position in the rear. "Percy, my good friend Andrew Jackson would like to make your acquaintance, and I think it would be wise if we kept my shooting prowess to ourselves." Percy took my twenty-dollar-bill and discreetly slipped it into his waders. "Mum's the word," he said.

"How'd you do?" shouted the president. Proudly, I held up a sampling of my limit. Relief swept over his face. "Wonderful. Wonderful. I'm sure the members will be interested to hear about your hunt."

Over roast duck, I described each of Percy's shots as if they were my own. The members were particularly interested in how I had doubled up on the teal. "That's one hell of a shot," the portly industrialist from Cleveland said. "I'm glad you figured out your lead."

That afternoon, the Club voted unanimously to accept Mike Wright's plan. Today, the peninsula is one of the crown jewels in the Canadian Wildlife Refuge System. The refuge itself is named after one of Canada's great sportsmen and conservationists. Only I know that it should be named after Mike Wright and Percy. It was Mike Wright's plan and Percy's shooting that saved it.

Diplomatic Immunity

IN THE FALL OF 1975, Dr. Robert Jenkins, the Conservancy's top scientist and most vocal proponent of the preservation of biotic diversity, made an unexpected pronouncement. "Henceforth," said the Doc, "the Conservancy will no longer haphazardly acquire little lifeboats of diversity. We shall protect entire biological systems."

This change of focus resulted in a major turn for the Conservancy. Originally, Doc Jenkins had envisioned building our Ark from the scraps of natural areas that were left lying around after development: a hemlock gully here, a desert spring there, a patch of prairie in between. Now the Doc had decided that saving these little lifeboats of diversity was not the answer, because they would eventually be swamped by the ever-surging waves of growth. What we needed were luxury liners.

The Doc's diagnosis was undoubtedly influenced by the work of his contemporaries, most notably Professor Paul Ehrlich. Professor Ehrlich was quickly emerging as a principal defender of the environment. His books covered the entire spectrum of environmental issues: *The Population Bomb; The Race Bomb; How to Survive Affluence; Ark*

II; Population, Resources, Environment; and *Ecoscience* were just a sampling of his numerous publications. His shingle hung conspicuously near the top of Stanford's Ivory Tower; yet unlike most scientists, Ehrlich could explain the dangers facing the environment to the man on the street. He had an easy, outgoing style that worked well on TV. He was becoming a regular on Johnny Carson. No one could yuk up the environment like Ehrlich.

Doc Jenkins' style was more scientific, dogmatic, and territorial. He often had trouble articulating why it was important to preserve biotic diversity, even to members of the Conservancy. It was predictable that he would be taken aback when the board invited Professor Ehrlich to speak at one of our meetings. Worse yet, the professor took that particular opportunity to lecture the Conservancy on the proper way to preserve biotic diversity. Ehrlich warned that his studies at Stanford had proven conclusively that most small, isolated biological communities, both plant and animal, had little chance for survival without the support of surrounding ecosystems. Moreover, if one species in a small community were lost through either a natural calamity or human intervention, it could lead to the loss of dependent populations. "A cascading series of extinctions could quickly reduce the diversity in any small preserve plot," the professor intoned. "If the goal is to save biological diversity, the major focus must be on conserving entire ecosystems!"

The Doc, like any good Harvard man, was quick to expand on a competitor's research. It was not long after our meeting with Ehrlich that the Doc recruited a whole new crew of specialists. He gave them the rank of "preserve designer" and ordered them to identify the best remaining natural systems left in America. "Forget the scraps; bigger is better!"

Soon these young eager-beaver biologists were drawing lines

around millions of acres. The Doc installed a bank of computers whose sole function was to spit out reams of biological information. Biological scorecards were set up for each state. "No Conservancy project," he warned, "will be approved by the science department unless it is part of a pre-identified biological system."

Those of us involved in land acquisition were shocked. We were having enough trouble trying to buy the lifeboats. How were we ever going to pay for luxury liners?

After a heated debate and a realistic review of our resources, we settled on a course of action. We would focus on the protection of relatively undeveloped islands. Consequently, almost all of the Virginia Barrier Islands, most of the Golden Isles of Georgia, Little Traverse Island in Lake Michigan, more than three dozen islands off the coast of Maine, Dog Island in Apalachicola Bay, and large parts of the San Juan Islands in Puget Sound were protected by the Conservancy in the late 1970s. Most of these preserves were more than lifeboats; a few, like Parramore and Ossabaw, were legitimate luxury liners. Then in early 1978, we were presented with the Queen Mary of natural areas: Santa Cruz Island.

The Doc was ecstatic. Santa Cruz, largest of the Channel Islands, was practically within the shadow of Stanford's Ivory Tower and just fifty miles from Burbank, home of "The Tonight Show." Except for a small ranch house and some jeep trails, the island was totally undeveloped. Fortunately, the family that owned more than 90 percent of Santa Cruz was conservation-minded, wanted to see the island preserved, and, due to a death in the family, had to sell. The National Park Service was interested, but the family did not want the island to go to public ownership. It was afraid that, being so close to Los Angeles, the island would be overrun with tourists if it were turned into a national park. The family wanted to see Santa Cruz forever managed as a natural preserve, a living remnant of what Southern California must have been like before the white man arrived bearing freeways and tinsel.

Henry Little, the director of The Nature Conservancy's western regional office, was captain of the Santa Cruz project. It was his job to put the deal together and steer it through our board of governors. After long and complex negotiations, the family finally agreed to sell the island to the Conservancy for the bargain price of $2.5 million. That was already more money than we had ever raised privately for an acquisition, but $2.5 million was just the start. Henry estimated that we would need another $1.5 million as an endowment to manage the preserve. The reason that we needed to raise such a large endowment was that we would have to eradicate 30,000 feral sheep.

During the 1950s, the family had started a hunt club as a way of generating some extra income for Santa Cruz. The club's membership was composed of well-heeled sportsmen from L.A. who would pay a fat fee to motor out to the island and pop a few feral sheep. The club worked fine for a while; but as the membership got older, it became obvious that the rugged terrain of Santa Cruz was more suited to the sheep than to the elderly hunters. The club members did less and less hunting. The only sheep that were shot were the ones too old or too stupid to stay away from the ranch house. The young, smart, virile sheep were free to reproduce to their hearts' content.

Sheep are frequent fornicators. By 1978, there were 30,000 feral sheep industriously munching away on our biotic diversity. That number was growing exponentially. If left unchecked, the sheep would soon have Santa Cruz, this last remnant of native Southern California, looking like the surface of the moon.

The Doc had undertaken an exhaustive study of the sheep problem. Ecologically, there was no question that the sheep had to go. Here was a classic case of one very common animal threatening to destroy a treasure chest of endangered species. The Doc's study showed that there were forty-two plant species on Santa Cruz that were found only on the Channel Islands. These plants had been evolving for centuries, and since there were no grazing animals indigenous to the Channel Islands, they had never developed natural defense systems. Unlike plants of the same genus on the mainland, Santa Cruz's flora have no spines, stickers, poisons, coarse textures, bad tastes, or any of the other defenses characteristic of their mainland cousins. The sheep loved them. Biologists labeled them the "ice cream plants." "So what?" the man on the street might ask. "The sheep are just doing what comes naturally. Too bad for the plants. Isn't that nature—survival of the fittest? Besides, sheep are warm and cuddly. What good are these plants?"

The answer, of course, is, "What good are you?" No species can survive by itself. Our world is dependent on biotic diversity. Who knows how these forty-two plants might help us in the future? Agronomists had already discovered that plants on Santa Cruz are far more drought-resistant than similar plants on the mainland. This characteristic might become extremely important, especially as our planet enters a new warming cycle. It was entirely conceivable that a plant from Santa Cruz might make it possible to save millions of people in Africa from starvation.

Removing the sheep from Santa Cruz was going to be a very sensitive issue. We had looked at everything from Scottish sheepdogs to Navajo shepherds. All were prohibitively expensive, and none guaranteed satisfactory results. In fact, we discovered that a humane society that had offered to remove the sheep at an exorbitant price actually had a contract with a dog food company. The only feasible alternative was to pick the very best of the Conservancy's land stewards, arm them with high-powered rifles, and have them put down the sheep as quickly and painlessly as possible.

It was a hard decision for the staff. Raising $4 million was one thing; that's what nonprofit organizations were supposed to do. Slaughtering 30,000 feral sheep was something else. What conservation organization engaged in genocide? But if the goal was to preserve an entire, unique biological system, it was senseless to buy the island unless we were committed to getting rid of the sheep.

The Santa Cruz project was scheduled to be presented to our board at the May 1978 meeting. But Santa Cruz was such an important project that we decided to bring the board to the island. Once we got them on board the Queen Mary, we hoped that its sheer size would overshadow the issues of money and sheep. Overshadowed or not, these issues were still going to be problems.

We figured that we would need a lead grant of at least $1 million if we hoped to receive approval from the board to purchase the island. It seemed impossible that we would be able to raise that amount of money. Northern Californians were the ones who gave to conservation, but they didn't like Southern California. They considered everything south of Santa Barbara to be a wasteland and resented squandering the state's precious water—most of which comes from the north—on swimming pools and golf courses. There was little interest in conservation in Southern California. Big money went to Palm Springs and Vegas, not to conservation. Northern Californians would have liked to turn off the tap and watch Southern California wither into desert.

Fortunately, Henry Little had unearthed an heiress from New England who had recently migrated to San Francisco. This heiress was a very interesting young woman. She had graduated with honors from the Yale School of Forestry and was committed to conservation. Despite her conservative upbringing, she was a free spirit who found the Northeast physically overdeveloped and mentally confining. She liked the openness of the West and had indicated that she would like to do something significant for California. Henry enthusiastically described the enormous potential of Santa Cruz. He gave the heiress a copy of the Doc's report. She was intrigued. Eradicating the sheep didn't bother her. She understood the concept of biotic diversity, and, just as important, she didn't care that people from Northern California did not ordinarily give to projects in Southern California. She was her own person. She would do what she damn well pleased.

Henry invited the heiress to accompany the board to the island. He assigned Spencer Beebe as her escort. Spencer was one of the Conservancy's best deal makers and fundraisers. Unlike most Conservancy deal makers, Spencer actually knew something about nature. More importantly, he could use nature to excite donors. Spencer was forever picking up snakes and finding baby birds. I once saw him present a potential donor with a young raptor. While the bird froze the donor with an icy glare, Spencer pounced on his pockets. Together, they plucked the donor clean.

But like any of us, Spencer wasn't perfect. He liked to raise money for anything having to do with conservation. He might start out asking a donor for $100,000 for a prairie in eastern Oregon and end up with $500,000 for a study of brown bears in Alaska. So Henry assigned me to chaperone Spencer and keep him focused on Santa Cruz. Henry was counting on Spencer to obtain a lead grant of $1 million from the heiress. That would take care of our immediate money problem.

As for the sheep, we all knew that the approval of our plan would hinge on the vote of the Ambassador. The Ambassador was a very proper career diplomat, a longtime board member, and the self-appointed chief of protocol for the Conservancy. He had one approach to every issue: How would it affect our image? If we could persuade the Ambassador that the sheep must go, he would persuade the rest of the board. After all, what were ambassadors for, if not to explain difficult situations? We knew that the Ambassador would make an in-depth tour of the island before casting his vote. He liked to know all of the facts, and he wouldn't be intimidated by the rugged terrain. He had spent a good deal of time hiking through the Swiss Alps.

Henry assigned his old friend, Tom Macy, to guide the Ambassador. Tom was a former Marine officer who had served in Vietnam with Henry, and, like the Ambassador, Tom was in tremendous shape. Henry instructed Tom to show the Ambassador the damage the sheep were doing, even if it meant chasing them through every ravine and crevice on Santa Cruz. Tom's mission was to so prejudice the Ambassador against the sheep that he would vote to do what was right rather than what seemed socially correct. If the Ambassador supported annihilation, that would take care of our sheep problem.

Everything seemed promising as we boarded our boat to the island. It was a beautiful May day, sunny but pleasant thanks to an offshore breeze. Spencer started working on the heiress right away. It was not a tough assignment. Just as we expected, she was bright and sincerely interested in nature. She was also extremely attractive and very informal. She wrote down the birds that Spencer identified. I interrupted only once, when a pod of whales swam by. Spencer immediately took a new tack and started talking about a friend who had a plan to save the whales, if only he could find a few million. Fortunately, the whales sounded and I was able to get Spencer back on course.

Henry had arranged a sumptuous picnic lunch at the ranch. Local treats like abalone and calamari were washed down with fine California wine. After lunch, Henry made a detailed presentation of the financial and management problems that we faced. Then the Doc rose to exhort the board. "If our goal is to save biological diversity, the major focus must be on conserving entire ecosystems. Bigger is better; and once the sheep are gone, we will have saved nothing bigger and better than Santa Cruz."

Henry encouraged us all to explore the island before the board took its final vote. Most of the board members and staff were content to sit in the warm sun and watch some old sheep nibble on the flora. A few, like the Ambassador and Macy, set out in pursuit of nature. I would have preferred to stay behind, but I dutifully tagged along when Spencer invited the heiress to go for a hike. Spencer guided us up a jeep trail that led to the highest ridge on the island. It was a tough walk but well worth the effort. From the top, we could see all of Santa Cruz and the distant haze of L.A. A flock of sheep came scampering over the next ridge. The Ambassador and Macy were close on their heels. The Ambassador, striding purposefully, gave us a hearty hello and headed down into the adjacent ravine. Macy looked at us, shook his head, mopped his brow, and tromped off in pursuit.

We could see the Pacific lapping the shore below. After our heavy exertion under a hot sun, it looked cool and refreshing. "Let's go for a swim," said Spencer. "Great idea," echoed the heiress.

"I don't know," I said. "It could be quite a hike. This trail seems to wind all over the island."

"We'll go straight down this ravine," Spencer said. He kicked off his shoes and sprinted down the grassy slope. The heiress immediately followed. I reluctantly tailed after them.

Descending the ravine proved to be a mistake. The grassy slope soon steepened and led to jagged rocks. It was heavy going. Spencer would never have admitted it, but he shouldn't have left his shoes. The sheep had denuded all of the vegetation, the soil had eroded, and the protruding rocks were cutting his feet. We kept pushing on. The lower we got, the hotter it got. There was no breeze in the ravine and no cover from the midday sun. We were glad to find a little pool of water. We stopped to splash our faces and let Spencer soak his feet.

I was startled when the heiress took off her blouse, dipped it into the pool, and tied it around her head. Then she slipped out of her slacks, soaked them in the water, and tied them around her waist. Spencer looked equally startled. "Um, let's keep moving," he stammered. "We're almost to the beach." He hobbled forward while the heiress strode behind, clad only in her bra and panties. I brought up the rear. I was sorely disappointed when we finally reached the beach. Following the heiress had given me the inspiration to carry on. "Quick, over here!" Spencer yelled over the pounding surf. Ever alert, he had spotted a bird washed up on the beach. "Let's catch it!" He took off down the sand, and I ran after him. The bird saw us coming. Though it waddled awkwardly toward the sea, it was too slow. Spencer grabbed it.

"It's a surf scooter," he told me as he flipped it over. "See, its feet are so far back on its body that it can't take off on land." I must have looked confused. "Like a loon," he continued. "Good for swimming but terrible on land. This guy must have gotten washed up by a big wave."

We turned to look at the waves, but our eyes never reached the water. They froze on the heiress. She was walking toward us, stark naked. "Oh, no. Now what?" I heard Spencer mumble under his breath.

Obviously the heiress had shed her New England heritage. She was now a free-spirited Californian. "Hey," Spencer said, trying to act nonchalant, "here's a sea scooter for you." It was the old 'give the donor the bird' trick, only this donor had no pockets for Spencer to pick clean. The heiress fondled the little fellow. "I was just showing Dave how its feet are so far back on its body that it can't walk on land." Spencer started to reach for the bird, but then pulled back his hand. "Ahh," he said awkwardly, "if you flip it over, you can see its feet." The heiress did as she was instructed. I tried to focus on the scooter but the heiress's ample assets got in the way.

I felt a strong need to get in the water. "Let's go for a swim," I suggested. "Yeah," Spencer quickly concurred. We both stripped down to our Patagonias. Most old-line Conservancy employees wear Patagonia shorts instead of underwear when they go into the field. Experience has shown that Patagonia shorts can get you through almost anything. You can run in them, swim in them, hike in them, climb in them, or even sleep in them. The preferred color is oak-leaf green.

Spencer and I dove through the surf trying not to stare at the heiress as she assisted the scooter over the waves. We all paddled out beyond the surf and watched as the scooter flapped its way to freedom. The cool blue Pacific felt good. It revitalized us and soothed our battered bodies.

We were surprised to see Macy and the Ambassador come swimming along the shore toward us. They were both using the modified Australian crawl, a popular stroke for serious long-distance swimmers. The Ambassador had to be crowding sixty, but he was still plenty game. He was keeping up with Macy. The Ambassador swam right into us. He pulled up with a start. "Say, pleasant day for a dip, isn't it?"

We all treaded water and chatted for a while. The Ambassador was entertaining the heiress with tales of his hike. I wondered what he would say if he knew that the attractive young woman bobbing in the water a few yards from him was totally naked. I hoped I would never find out. Swimming with a nude major donor could not possibly fit the Conservancy's image.

Macy swam in to shore and began prying mussels from the rocks. "Anybody hungry?" he hollered, holding up a handful.

"Say, Pacific mussels on the half shell. They're the best. Have you ever tried them?" the Ambassador asked the heiress.

"Oh, we prefer clams in New England, but Pacific mussels do sound special," she replied.

Spencer and I looked at each other. Here was more trouble. If the heiress got out of the water, she probably would throw the Ambassador for such a loop that he would never again want to hear the words "Santa Cruz." The Ambassador was anything but "California Casual." The only way that we could cover her nudity was to keep the heiress in the water until the Ambassador left.

"Gee," said Spencer, "we were just about to swim out to, uh, to, uh. . ." Spencer gazed at the empty sea. "To those rocks over there," I interjected, pointing to a promontory far down the beach. "Right," Spencer added. "That's where we're sure to see some sea lions."

"Nonsense," the Ambassador scoffed. "We just came from there. There are no sea lions. The Conservancy staff are such kidders," he said knowingly to the heiress. "Let's sample the local delicacies."

"Come and get 'em!" yelled Macy. He was holding up another handful of mollusks. I could have killed him. Obviously, he had no idea of the predicament we faced.

That was all it took. The Ambassador and the heiress turned toward shore. Spencer and I looked at each other again. We were sunk. We braced for what we knew was about to be one of the most embarrassing moments in the history of The Nature Conservancy.

They caught the same wave and came popping out of the surf like a couple of penguins. "Oh, my God!" exclaimed Spencer. I rubbed my eyes in disbelief. There was the Ambassador, emerging from the water, looking quite proper but totally in the buff. Where was his bathing suit? Macy, draped in the standard Patagonia shorts, was so stunned that he dropped his mussels.

As usual, Spencer was quick to recover. "Come on," he said, "it's time to sell the island."

"What about our suits?" I asked.

"Leave them on," said Spencer. "The Ambassador is covered by diplomatic immunity."

When we emerged, the Ambassador, the heiress, and Macy were

leaning on the rocks eating mussels. The Ambassador was telling old war stories. Were it not for his attire, he could have been at a lawn party at the embassy.

The Ambassador borrowed Macy's Swiss Army knife, expertly shucked a mussel, and offered it to the heiress. She lapped it from its shell. I shuffled from foot to foot and discreetly glanced at the Ambassador. Miraculously, he was maintaining his composure.

It was getting late. Spencer was right; it was time to sell the island. "So, what about the sheep?" I asked the Ambassador. "Do you think we can handle that problem?"

"They've got to go!" he said unequivocally. "They are destroying the island. I intend to make that recommendation most emphatically."

"That's great, but we still need a lead grant of at least a million if we hope to exercise the option," stated Spencer. He looked directly at the heiress. "Can you help?"

She took another mussel, arched her neck, and let it slide slowly down her throat. "I'll commit $500,000 up front and another $500,000 to finish it off. That ought to give you enough to start and a strong challenge to raise the balance."

With that, she bounded back into the surf. "Hear, hear," exclaimed the Ambassador. "It seems we have a project. Nice work, gentlemen."

There was an awkward silence. "Ah, just one question, Ambassador," I asked. "What happened to your suit?"

The Ambassador assumed his most diplomatic stance. *"Honi soit qui mal y pense,"* he said, throwing open his arms to emphasize his nudity. He dove through the surf and began crawling his way back down the shore.

Spencer shook his head. "What does that mean?"

That evening, the Ambassador, immaculately garbed in a monogrammed blue blazer and club tie, stood before the full board of The

Nature Conservancy and pronounced sentence on the sheep. The heiress, attired sedately in a green-and-white cotton dress, formalized her pledge to Santa Cruz. The vote was unanimous. Henry, thanks in large part to a major grant from Arco, raised the rest of the money, and the island was purchased. Today, the sheep are almost gone. The native flora are flourishing. Santa Cruz is becoming the Queen Mary of natural areas. The Doc was right; bigger is better!

Footnote: In 1349, King Edward III was dancing with the Countess of Salisbury at a great court ball. Quite unexpectedly, the countess lost her garter. As the king, always the gentleman, bent over to pick it up, he saw several persons smile and indulge in snide remarks. This made the king angry, and he exclaimed, *"Honi soit qui mal y pense"* (Evil be to him who thinks evil).

The king slipped the garter onto his own leg and went on to say, presumably in English, that he would "make the garter so glorious that everyone would wish to wear it." He thus founded the Order of the Garter, which is the highest and the oldest order of knighthood in Great Britain. Its emblem is a dark blue garter, edged in gold, on which is printed the expression I heard for the first time from the Ambassador on that successful day in May.

Negotiations

DURING THE LATE SEVENTIES, The Nature Conservancy did some of the biggest land deals in the history of conservation. We acquired and protected places like Santa Cruz Island in California, the Santee Hunt Club in South Carolina, the Old Mashomack Hunt Club on Shelter Island, New York, the Pascagoula River bottomlands in Mississippi, Ossabaw Island in Georgia, and just about all of the Virginia barrier islands. There was no secret to our success. We knew what we wanted and had the financial ability to acquire it. Plus, we were ethical in our dealings and always tried to be nice to people.

We seldom publicized our deals. Some of our best projects were supported by donors who preferred to remain anonymous. They didn't want to be hounded by other nonprofits, and they didn't want their names associated with the conservation movement. This necessary low profile puzzled many within the environmental community. People assumed we knew things that they didn't, that we were withholding vital information.

When I became vice-president for land acquisition, I began to receive invitations to conferences and workshops hosted by other conservation groups. They called me an expert in land acquisition. They were hoping I would reveal our secrets. I politely declined. I knew I was no expert, and I told them that I honestly didn't think I had much to offer. These refusals only added to the Conservancy's mystique.

In September of 1979 I finally got caught. Jon Roush, a good friend and member of the Conservancy's national board of governors, asked me to attend a workshop in Jackson Hole. It was being hosted by a new nonprofit organization that Jon had helped form to assist citizen groups involved in the natural-resource issues confronting the northern Rockies. Shale oil, timbering, and mining were threatening the environmental integrity of this pristine area. The workshop was titled "Negotiations." When I told Jon that I honestly didn't think I had much to offer, his response was, "You'll be surprised."

I've never liked Jackson Hole. It's a very phony place. Everyone walks like a cowboy, talks like a cowboy, and looks like a cowboy, but nobody is a cowboy. No real cowboy could afford to live in Jackson Hole. Land prices have skyrocketed. The real cowboys have been stampeded by dudes in designer jeans and Tony Lama boots who clip coupons from bonds. Big bonds.

Even the famous Jackson Hole Elk Hunt is a sham. When the valley floor was taken over by urban cowboys, the U.S. Fish and Wildlife Service had to set up a refuge for the elk: The Jackson Hole National Elk Refuge, encompassing less than a thousand acres, is all that is left of the herd's winter range. Once they leave the high country, the majestic elk go on welfare. They mill around their little refuge waiting for the Fish and Wildlife Service to hand out bales of hay. When the herd gets "too large," the Service authorizes another famous Jackson Hole Elk Hunt. A "hunter" lucky enough to win the lottery is issued a permit that allows him to ride out on the feeding sled and pop an elk. This is about as sporting as shooting a barnyard cow. Cowboys, elk refuges, hunters; nothing is real in Jackson Hole.

The workshop was being held at the Triple X, a well-known dude ranch some forty miles north of town. I was surprised that there was no one to meet me when I arrived at the airport. A cab would have destroyed Fitzie's travel budget, so I walked out to the John D. Rockefeller, Jr., Memorial Parkway and stuck out my thumb. Two guys in a shiny new pickup stopped. They were wearing crisp, clean ten-gallon hats and had the standard high-powered rifle hanging in the gun rack. "Where ya headin'?" they asked.

"A place called the Triple X," I said. The driver nodded and pointed to the back of the truck.

There was a nip in the air, but I was warmed by the midday sun as I lay in the bed of the truck. I looked up at the Tetons, ablaze with golden aspen. We crossed crystal-clear streams which sparkled as they danced toward the Snake River.

Even the caravans of motor homes going to and from Grand Teton National Park could not detract from the natural beauty all around me. If ever a place deserved protection, it was the Grand Teton Valley. I was disappointed when the pickup pulled up to the entrance of the Triple X. I wanted to keep going. It was too nice a day to be inside talking about the environment when I could have been outside experiencing it.

I climbed out of the truck, grabbed my bag, dusted off my sport jacket, and looked up at the entrance to the Triple X. It was the classic two log posts with a crossed beam from which hung the XXX brand. I could see what looked like the main ranch house half a mile or so up the dirt road. I started walking.

The reception desk was deserted. I heard a lot of yelling coming from behind a door marked "Conference Room." Evidently the workshop had started without me. True to my Conservancy training, I decided to avoid the controversy and moseyed out to the stables.

I had a reason: That very night Larry Holmes was defending his WBC heavyweight championship against Ken Norton, and I wanted to find a TV. I figured that the rest of the workshop would have little interest in the fight. Most environmentalists, while continually seeking confrontation on complex issues, have no time for something as simple and straightforward as the heavyweight championship of the world. A ranch hand who mucked out the stables wouldn't be burdened by the natural-resource issues confronting the northern Rockies. He'd be a fight fan for sure.

I was wrong. The guy I found down at the stables was leaning back in a chair, his well-worn boots propped up on a bale of hay. He was sucking on a piece of grass. His dirty ten-gallon hat was tilted down over his dirty, unshaven face. His eyes moved contemptuously from my Weejuns to my argyle socks, up my corduroys to my gold-buttoned blue blazer. "How ya doin'?" I asked.

He slowly withdrew the grass from his mouth. "What can I do for ya, podner?" He looked and sounded like a real cowboy, an endangered species in Jackson Hole.

"You got a TV in this place?"

He sat up in his chair, pointed the piece of grass at me and scowled accusingly. "Podner, yew want tennis courts, a golf course, and a swimmin' pool, you've come to the wrong place. This here's a ranch."

Ranch? Who did this guy think he was kidding? There hadn't been a real steer at the Triple X since John D. Rockefeller, Jr., was in his prime.

"Yeah, and you're the Lone Ranger."

The piece of grass fell from his hand as he clenched it into a fist. Fortunately, he remained seated.

"I didn't ask for tennis courts, a golf course, or a pool," I continued. "All I asked for was one lousy TV so I could watch the heavyweight championship of the world along with forty million other Americans."

He looked me hard in the eye. "Well, podner, we ain't got that either."

So much for Holmes versus Norton.

The workshop was breaking up when I got back to the main house. Someone called out, "Hey, Dave, where have you been?" It was Jon Roush.

I told him about my altercation with the real cowboy. "Don't worry," he said. "You won't have time for any fights. We'll be working all night."

He then introduced me to the conference facilitator, an intense young man who looked far too preoccupied with natural-resource issues to worry about meeting somebody at the airport. "Oh. So glad you finally got here," he said, as if my being late were my fault. "You missed the first session, but no harm, we're just getting ready to introduce the resource people."

"That's wonderful," I replied, "Only I have no idea what I'm supposed to do."

"Oh. Didn't you get a packet describing the workshop?"

"No," I said, a little testily. After flying two thousand miles, bumming in from the airport, and arguing with the Lone Ranger, I was starting to get upset. "I've gotten nothing."

"Oh. Here, take my copy." He handed me a tacky little brochure entitled "Negotiating Resource Policy" and then yelled, "Everybody back into the conference room."

I was swept up in a wave of eager environmentalists. Soon the room was packed. Most of the guys had beards; the women had long, straight hair. Their dress could best be described as Western Casual:

boots, Levis, chamois shirts, heavy wool sweaters, and down vests. No loafers, ties, or blazers—this group looked even less businesslike than I had expected. I tried to hide myself in a corner.

The conference facilitator clanged an old cowbell and called for order. It took him a while to settle everyone down. They were charged for action. The first session must have been a barnburner. I wondered what they had been talking about. I glanced at my brochure; there was no agenda.

"Now, it gives me great pleasure to introduce our resource people," the facilitator told the crowd. "These are the experts. These are the people who have the knowledge we need. Listen to them and learn! After we hear from our resource people, it will be time to play The Game!" The facilitator announced "The Game" as if it were Christmas morning. Someone gave a loud "yahoo!" I couldn't believe it.

The facilitator gestured for silence. He introduced the first resource person, an old codger from the American Arbitration Association. He was pretty spry for an ancient arbitrator. He sprang to his feet and launched into a harangue on how "ours is a culture of confrontation. Good guys finish last. Winning is what counts." Yadda, yadda, yadda. "But to be a winner, a skillful negotiator has to look for opportunities to compromise. . . ."

Finally he wound down: "Through consensus, one achieves better solutions! Give a little, but get a lot!" He sat down. There was polite applause. I disagreed with his emphasis on confrontation, but what else could be expected from the American Arbitration Association?

The facilitator thanked the ancient arbitrator, and then introduced a short, dumpy, unhappy-looking woman. She was the founding president of some group having to do with women in labor. I looked down at my brochure. It noted that her work emphasized "the common issues of the feminist, conservation, and labor movements." I wondered what issues feminists, conservationists, and unionists possibly could have in common. She wasted no time in letting me know.

"I am in total disagreement with compromise! Women have always been compromised! Conservation has always been compromised! And labor has always been compromised! Yadda, yadda, yadda. "Struggle is the essence of life! We must struggle and fight for our existence! We must struggle and fight for our very lives! We are all adversaries at the bargaining table." Et cetera.

"Our enemies change, but the battle is ongoing! Feminists, conservationists, and the labor movement must keep fighting until we have won an unconditional VIC-TOOOR-Y!! We must *never* compromise!" The woman threw her hands into the air with her fingers spread in a V. She resembled a short, dumpy, unhappy Richard Nixon. There was a thunderclap of applause.

What have I gotten myself into? One more speech like that, and the FBI would round us all up. The facilitator was clanging his cowbell. The air was charged with anticipation. And with good reason. The next resource person was a militant young labor organizer. He had a ponytail, a flowing moustache, and a motorcycle jacket. He was trouble.

"I have come here to praise conflict, not to bury it," he intoned in a sepulchral chant. "I believe that conflict is inevitable, and healthy. It is a fact that in our society, power is unequally distributed." Yadda, yadda, yadda. "In our society, there are the have's and the have-not's." His voice started to rise. "For the have-not's to achieve power, they must alter their relationship with those in power. That involves conflict!" There was a scattering of applause. "We must not be afraid to break the rules! Rules are made by those in power to protect their power! Once we have the power, we will make the rules!" I started wondering whether I was in The Rockies or The Urals.

"If there is to be a successful revolution, we must be willing to break the self-serving rules of those who seek to keep us disenfranchised, those who seek to keep us enslaved to their power!" He paused for the spirited applause he knew was coming. He was a real pro. "I AM NOT CONCERNED WITH THE RIGHT SOLUTION!!" he screamed, thrusting a clenched fist into the air. "I AM CONCERNED WITH POWER!" The crowd went wild. They rose to their feet, waving their fists and chanting, "Power! Power! Power!"

This guy deserved the Order of Lenin. I looked toward the door. Where was Jon Roush? We had to get out of there. This was no place for The Nature Conservancy. The facilitator was clanging his cowbell in a frenzy. "Please! Please! Please sit down! Please, may I have your attention! The best is yet to come!" People began to settle back into their seats.

"And now, our final expert!" the facilitator stated with great excitement. "Here is a warrior who's actually done it, a warrior who's gone toe to toe with the captains of industry, a warrior who has faced power and seized it for conservation! Representing The Nature Conservancy, from Washington, D.C., the capital of power, David Morine!"

The crowd started turning in their seats. Where was this mythic hero, this David who had taken on the Goliaths of corporate America? I stood in the corner, twiddling the gold buttons on my blazer. What could I conceivably say to these fanatics?

"Gee, it sure is nice to be here," I mumbled. "I am pleased to have this opportunity to meet with all of you." I recognized my voice, but I couldn't believe it was me talking. "I'm afraid that at The Nature Conservancy we approach our business a little differently. We don't like conflict. We don't like confrontation. We always try to be nice to people, especially people in power. We think that most of them are basically okay, that they want to do what's right. We always try to be ethical, we try to understand their positions, we look for reasonable alternatives. We work for the best possible solutions."

I could feel the electricity draining from the room. "The concept of environmental warriors battling captains of industry is not valid for the Conservancy. We find we save a lot more land working with industry than by fighting with it. We use the tax code to forge partnerships with corporations and individuals who have the power to make decisions affecting significant natural areas.

"We have learned that to save our natural resources, we must deal ethically and effectively with the people who control them. That's the secret to The Nature Conservancy's success."

I expected at least a businesslike round of applause. There was nothing. People were staring at me as though I came from another planet.

The facilitator came to my rescue. "Thank you, Dave," he said, somewhat condescendingly. "The Conservancy certainly has a novel approach to conservation." Then to the crowd, "Let's take a ten-minute break before the game."

At the mention of the game, the participants forgot about me altogether. They buzzed excitedly as they moved into the corridor. I was totally ignored except for Jon Roush. He came over looking very much amused.

"See, I told you you'd be surprised," he said gleefully.

"I can't wait for the game. What is it, a public lynching?"

"You'll see," said Jon, still smiling.

The game was called "Operation Wilderness: The Ultimate in Environmental Conflicts." The participants were divided into four groups: the Forest Service, a local timber company, residents of the town, and the environmentalists. The object of "Operation Wilderness" was to hammer out an agreement satisfactory to all parties regarding the use of 800,000 acres of timberland located just sixty miles from an urban area of one million people. Historically it provided hunting and fishing opportunities for the townspeople, recreational land for city people, and logs for the local timber company. Now the demands for more recreational land for people from the city and more timber for the local mill were causing a conflict. The Forest Service, which managed the land for the federal government, had to adopt a long-term management plan for the area. It hoped to bring all the interested parties together and have them work out an agreement.

The final agreement had to allow:

- the local timber company to remain prosperous;
- the Forest Service to carry out its mandate of multiple use;
- the townspeople to remain employed, yet still have enough land for hunting and fishing; and
- the environmentalists to preserve as much land as possible for wilderness and passive outdoor recreation.

Each group was given "negotiating units" consisting of deeds to certain plots of land, money, and political influence, but they were not divided equally, and no group knew what the others had. A resource person had been assigned to coach each group. Naturally, I got the environmentalists. Given my introductory remarks, the environmentalists saw little need for my coaching.

I watched with great interest as each group staked out a corner of the conference room and busily went to work. A young warrior soon emerged as the leader of the environmentalists. "Power," he intoned in the now popular chant. "We must seize power."

"How can we seize power before we know who has it?" inquired an elderly gentleman in a Pendleton shirt, string tie, and hush puppies.

"We seem to have some political influence," he continued, thumbing through his material, "but what is that worth?"

No one had an answer. Nobody looked to me for guidance, but I saw this as a chance to volunteer my resources. "Why don't you walk around and ask the other groups what they've got?" I interjected. "You're all in the same boat. They might be willing to swap some information. At the very least, you'll get a feel for who's got what."

"Ask?" The young buck glared at me. "Warriors don't ask. They take."

No one came to my defense. It was obvious the group was upset that they had pulled such a dud for a resource. Even the ancient arbitrator would have been better.

"Maybe we should consider some type of compromise," suggested a professorial pipe-smoking fellow.

"Compromise?" snorted the gray-haired mate of the elderly gentleman. "We must never compromise."

"Women, labor, and conservation have always been compromised," reiterated an aging hippie with large breasts hanging untethered beneath her turtleneck. "We must fight for an unconditional victory."

"But how much power do we have?" bleated a roly-poly little guy with Coke-bottle glasses and a toupee. "We could very well end up with nothing."

"That's true," reasoned the pipe-smoking professor. "We have little money, and no land. We should at least consider a compromise."

The young buck wasn't about to be compromised. "Power. We must seize power."

"But how?" demanded the elderly gentleman.

"You'd be the last to know," snapped his wife.

Yadda, yadda, yadda. I had never seen so much wasted energy. The group wrangled back and forth all afternoon. They hashed and rehashed their negotiating units. Who had the power? Was it the timber company, which was being advised by the union organizer, and probably had the money? The Forest Service, which was under the benign eye of the ancient arbitrator? They definitely had the land. Or the townspeople, who were being exhorted by the unhappy little woman? What did they have? Where was the power? To compromise, or not to compromise?

The other groups were starting to break for dinner. The timber company came lumbering by. They were all smiles. It was obvious they thought they had us stumped. The Forest Service looked hungry but content. They couldn't lose under their multiple-use mandate. The townspeople were actually chuckling. What Nixonian plot had they hatched? Only we environmentalists were gridlocked.

Finally the room fell silent. Everyone except us had already gone to dinner. The roly-poly little guy's stomach rumbled. "What do you think?" he asked, turning to me in desperation.

Finally, I had a chance to coach. "Seems to me that you can't develop a realistic strategy because you don't have enough information. You want to seize the power, but you can't even find it. All you have is some political influence, whatever that's worth. If you overreach, you could lose everything. The only way you can be sure of saving the maximum amount of wilderness is to know what chits the other groups control."

"That's obvious," countered the young warrior. "So what would Mr. Nature Conservancy do?"

It was time to put these warriors to the test. "I don't see why you're arguing. You need information. Well, there it is." I pointed around the room. "Everyone's gone. Go over and look at their notes. Find out what they have, then you can figure out exactly what to do. You'll blow their socks off."

Again, everyone looked at me as if I had come from another planet.

"Look," I continued in my best locker-room style. "In the real world, you try to get as much information as you can before you negotiate. Information is power. You've got the field to yourself. There's no rule that says you can't look at somebody else's notes if they're dumb enough to leave them lying around. Here's your chance. Go for it!"

The young warrior jumped to his feet. "Just who do you think you are?"

"Yeah," said the elderly gentleman.

"What are you trying to do?" demanded the buxom hippie, thrusting her breasts forward with great indignation. "That would wreck the game!"

Everyone else immediately agreed. It was the first time they had agreed on anything all afternoon. Apparently I had molded them into a team.

"Hey," I insisted, "don't you want to seize the power? Crush your opponents? Win the game?"

"Sure we want to win," protested the young warrior. "But we want to win fair and square."

"Frankly, I'm somewhat disappointed in The Nature Conservancy," said the pipe-smoking professor. "I thought you were an ethical organization that tried to be nice to people. This is not very ethical, or very nice."

"Let's eat," said the roly-poly little guy. Again, there was unanimity.

I didn't bother to stay for dinner. I grabbed my bag and hitched a ride back down the Parkway. I just made the last flight to Denver. The world heavyweight championship fight was on when I landed. I watched

Larry Holmes knock out Ken Norton in the eighth and caught the red-eye back to D.C.

I was able to sleep the whole way home. Conservation in the northern Rockies was going to be all right. The environmentalists had passed their test. They weren't crazed warriors, after all; they were ethical conservationists who wanted to do right. And eventually, they might even learn to be nice to people.

I Give Joy to Women

IN THE SUMMER OF 1980, Pat Noonan announced that he was going to step down as president of The Nature Conservancy. His resignation caught most people by surprise.

Pat came to see me shortly after his announcement. He told me that he had done what he wanted to do as president. During his six years at the helm, the Conservancy had become a major force in land conservation, had forged a unique relationship with the corporate community, and had completed its first capital campaign, an effort that raised $23 million and exceeded all goals. Pat felt it was time for him to move on to a new challenge.

"I've found a big foundation that wants to become active in conservation," he continued. "Its trustees are not your typical conservationists. They're hard-nosed businessmen. Their interest in the out-of-doors comes from hunting and fishing. They want to save land, but they don't want to deal with a bunch of fuzzy-faced idealists. They're not comfortable with most of the people in the conservation movement."

Pat had mentioned these trustees to me before, when they'd

made a modest grant to our capital campaign. For these guys, conservation was just another use of our natural resources, just another business. As the trustees saw it, if conservationists wanted to see an area protected, they shouldn't throw themselves in front of bulldozers and haul developers into court. They should step up, put their own money on the line, and buy it. They should compete in the open market with the timber companies, oil companies, mining companies, and developers. "Not-for-profits don't pay taxes!" the trustees were quick to point out. "What more do they want?"

"I think these guys are ready to make a real commitment to conservation," Pat said. "They like the way we've courted industry. They like our style. They've indicated that they want to see a major proposal from the Conservancy."

"Then, Pat," I asked, "why are you resigning?" It was the question everyone was asking.

"Simple," he told me. "To get these guys involved, we're going to have to concentrate on a few major projects. I can't work on projects if I'm running the organization." As usual, Pat was right on the money. "We need a major project. Think big. If you could do any project, what would it be?"

"Easy," I responded. "Bottomland hardwoods." My work on the Pascagoula River in Mississippi had convinced me that bottomland hardwoods were the most threatened natural system in America. "If we start right now, we might be able to save a few remnants."

"Great. Write it up," Pat concluded.

I sharpened my pencil and went to work. My proposal focused on five relatively undisturbed rivers that flowed into the Gulf of Mexico; the Pearl, the Mobile/Tensaw, the Choctawhatchee, the Apalachicola, and the Suwannee. These five rivers, along with the Pascagoula, were the lifeblood for the eastern half of the Gulf.

The introduction to my proposal waxed eloquent on how, in 1803, when Jefferson made the Louisiana Purchase, there were fifty million acres of bottomland hardwoods covering the Southeast; how by 1980 this system had been reduced to a mere 3.5 million acres (and that these remaining forests were being cleared and planted for soybeans at the rate of 300,000 acres a year); how bottomland hardwoods played a vital role in controlling floods and reducing water pollution; how over a million sportsmen hunted and fished along these rivers; how rare and endangered species like the sawback turtle, the Florida panther, and the swallowtailed kite, were hiding out, fugitives from development, in these bottomland hardwoods. Given the fact that I knew next to nothing about timbering, farming, hunting, fishing, and biology, I thought my introduction was excellent.

What I proposed was a million dollars of seed money for each river. With a $5-million grant, I figured that we could convince the Fish and Wildlife Service to create five new wildlife refuges along these rivers. We would save 150,000 acres of bottomland hardwoods, which would be by far the biggest land conservation program the Conservancy had ever undertaken.

Pat quickly scanned my proposal. "Hmm. Five rivers. Five new refuges. Seed money. Acreage. It's a start." He looked up. "Not bad. Scrap all this nature stuff in the introduction and throw in a couple of pictures of ducks. These guys know all they want to know about nature. What they want to see are pro formas. Show 'em how their money's gonna work. They're only gonna ask two questions: Where's the leverage, and where's the rollover?"

I resharpened my pencil and put together five pro formas, one of each river. Leverage and rollover flowed through my figures. We'd take a grant of $5 million over five years and use it as down payments on lands worth $15 million. That would be the leverage: three to one. Then we'd sell these lands to the Fish and Wildlife Service at our cost, recapture our $5 million, and roll it over into more down payments on another $15 million worth of land. Using this method, I projected that we'd save $30 million worth of land. At an average cost of $200 an acre, we could protect 150,000 acres over ten years. It would be a good deal for the foundation because we would be leveraging their grant six to one. It would be a good deal for the Fish and Wildlife Service because we'd be helping them set up five new refuges. It would be a good deal for the Conservancy because we'd be protecting bottomland hardwoods, an endangered system. Not bad, I thought. I was thinking big.

"Not big enough," said Pat. He took his pen and started scribbling. He kept mumbling figures to himself. "Fifteen million dollars. Roll their money twice, sounds good." Mumble. Mumble. "Three million dollars a year for five years. Times six to one. Ninety million. That's it," he pronounced happily. "You do good work."

"Pat," I asked, studying the chicken tracks all over my proposal. "What did I say?"

"Simple. Instead of asking for a grant of $5 million over five years, you're going to ask for $15 million over five years. That means . . ." Pat did another quick calculation. ". . . we'll be saving 450,000 acres of bottomland hardwoods. That should be big enough."

"Big enough! That's impossible! Where are we ever going to find that much land and that much money?"

Pat was unfazed. "Remember, to the swift belong the race." Pat often used this cornball expression to end a discussion.

On November 4, 1980, the foundation's trustees approved a grant of $15 million to the Conservancy's new Rivers of the Deep South program. It was the largest single grant ever made in the history of conservation. A check for $3 million was attached to the letter approving our proposal.

On November 6, 1980, Ronald Wilson Reagan was elected the

fortieth President of these United States. In January, 1981, he appointed the less-than-honorable James G. Watt as the forty-third Secretary of the Interior. Secretary Watt soon made it clear that he had no interest in protecting any more of the interior. In fact, he was a strong backer of the Sagebrush Rebellion, which would have turned millions of acres over to his fat-cat political cronies. Watt was adamant that the Department of the Interior would be buying no more land. So much for our five new Fish and Wildlife Refuges. I parked our $3 million in high-interest CDs and waited to see what was going to happen.

Things got worse. By February, Watt had not only refused to consider buying any more land, he had welshed on all of the prior commitments that had been made to the Conservancy by his predecessor, Pat's good friend Cecil Andrus. We were left holding $20 million worth of natural areas that we had preacquired. By reneging on these promises, Watt had singlehandedly wiped out the strong base Pat had built for the Conservancy with the capital campaign.

The final blow came in March when Watt abolished the Bureau of Outdoor Recreation, the federal agency that helped states purchase land with 50-percent matching federal funds. According to my pro formas, Florida, Alabama, and Mississippi were going to use some of these matching funds to buy bottomland hardwoods along the rivers. It now became painfully obvious that there wouldn't be federal funds of any kind flowing into the rivers of the deep South.

"Now what?" I asked Pat. By this time, Pat was serving as a consultant to the Conservancy and an adviser to the foundation. This was a unique relationship, especially suited to Pat. Both the Conservancy and the foundation trusted his judgment, respected his ability to get things done, and knew that they would be done right.

"You'd better come up with something," he told me. "The foundation's general counsel wants to take a trip south in April to see what's happening with their $3 million. He's only going to ask two questions."

"I know," I replied glumly. "Where's the leverage? Where's the rollover?"

This was not good news. The general counsel was the trustee who had promoted the relationship with the Conservancy. He felt responsible for making sure that we got the biggest bang for the foundation's buck. On the surface, he was a very pleasant man, calm, affable, mild-mannered, and consistently polite; but I knew that beneath this veneer he was as hard as steel. This Harvard-trained lawyer was the most focused individual I had ever met. Once he decided to do something, it got done. There was no excuse for failure. If our proposal said that we were going to save 450,000 acres over ten years, we were going to save 450,000 acres. The fact that the Feds had dropped out was irrelevant. The foundation had delivered their $3 million six months ago, so where was the first project?

I didn't have it. I had found some land, a 17,000-acre tract along the Pearl River in Mississippi that St. Regis was willing to sell for $3 million. The property had been appraised for $4.5 million, but St. Regis had agreed to take the difference as a charitable donation. That was when Watt screwed me. Without the Feds' money, there was no leverage and no rollover. My last hope was to convince the state of Mississippi to buy this tract on their own as a state wildlife management area.

I called Charlie Deaton. Charlie had been the chairman of the Mississippi House Appropriations Committee, a member of the Wildlife Heritage Committee, and was instrumental in preserving the Pascagoula. He was now the special counsel to the governor of Mississippi and a member of the Conservancy's national board.

"Charlie," I said, "we've got a problem." I could hear him chewing on his big cigar as I explained the situation. "St. Regis is willing to donate $1.5 million. Do you think you can get the legislature to appropriate $3 million? We'll use the foundation's grant to provide the interim financing at no cost to the state."

There was a long pause. "Now let me tell ya, it don't look good," he drawled. "Reagan's cut back on a lot moah than just land. He's hit education, health, you name it. Moah land's the last thang people down heah are thinkin' about."

"Charlie," I pleaded, "according to Pat, this foundation can carry land conservation through the eighties. But they're gonna drop us like a rock if we can't perform. We've gotta come up with a project."

More chewing noises accompanied another long pause. Charlie used his cigar the way a professor uses a pipe. Chewing on it gave him time to think.

"Y'all come on down," he finally said. "We'll get the govanuh to meet with the boy and see what we can do."

This was good news. Charlie, in his own way, was as focused as the foundation's general counsel. He wasn't going to wheel out the "govanuh" unless he thought the state was interested in acquiring the land. I was sure that he liked the idea of introducing the governor to a trustee of one of the largest foundations in America. The general counsel was the type of person every politician wanted to know. Plus, it would be a real coup for Mississippi to take the lead in the Rivers of the Deep South program.

"We'll have the governor sell the general counsel on Mississippi," I told Pat, "and the general counsel sell the governor on conservation. If they hit it off, we're golden. If not, we're dead."

Pat twiddled his fingers. "Hmm." He obviously didn't like the odds. "It's too bad they don't know each other. If only we could think of some way to break the ice."

"They're both lawyers. They're both about the same age. They both like hunting. I'll put them both in the same boat when we tour the property. What more can we do?"

"Hmm." Pat was still thinking. "That might be enough."

Our plan was for Pat, the general counsel, and me to meet Charlie, the governor, and the rest of the governor's entourage at a little airport near the St. Regis tract. From there, state troopers would drive us to the river where we'd link up with the St. Regis people for the tour.

Despite all that they did for the public, the trustees were very private people. They preferred to stay out of the limelight and directed publicity toward the organizations they supported. They tended to be very reserved with people they didn't know. It wasn't easy to break the ice with any of the trustees.

The general counsel was even more reserved than usual as we flew toward Bogalusa, Louisiana, the only town with an airport on the Pearl River. I thought he liked the deal we had structured with St. Regis but was skeptical about the State of Mississippi coughing up $3 million for conservation. He knew that the state had appropriated $15 million for the Pascagoula project, but that had been before Reagan's cutbacks. Landing in Bogalusa didn't help. As we circled the airport, the general counsel commented that Bogalusa was the toughest town in America, the home of the Ku Klux Klan. Pat raised his eyebrows. So far, we had broken no ice.

We arrived a few minutes before the governor. I waited anxiously as the governor's plane taxied up to the tarmac. It might have been a mistake bringing a Harvard lawyer to Bogalusa, Louisiana, to meet the governor of Mississippi.

Charlie was the first out of the plane, his swept-back silver hair blowing in the breeze. He stopped, squinted into the sun, put on his mirrored sunglasses, and lit up his ubiquitous big cigar. He looked like a Southern politician. A line of reporters trailed after him. I could tell that Charlie was using the tour to help sell the project.

Then came the governor. He didn't look like a Southern politician. He had short, dark hair, tortoise-shell glasses, and didn't smoke. He looked a lot like the general counsel. Maybe there was hope.

The press flocked around the general counsel. Having a representative of a major Northeastern foundation come to Mississippi was news. I was sure that the general counsel would direct all questions to Pat and me, but Pat had slipped away. He had seized this moment to collar the governor. "Governor," he asked, "do you have a gift for the general counsel?"

The governor didn't know what to make of this question. He was used to getting gifts, not giving them. "Why, er, of course we have something, don't we, Charlie?"

Charlie fiddled with his cigar. "Govanuh, we'll get him an ashtray from the plane. It's got the state seal on it."

"That'll be nice, but here," Pat said, producing a small gift-wrapped package. "Give him this first, and really build him up. This guy's got a big ego." Nothing could have been further from the truth. What was Pat up to?

The governor took the package and turned it over in his hands, looking for a clue. Before he could say anything, the general counsel walked up to meet him.

"Welcome to the great state of Mississippi," the governor proclaimed, pumping the general counsel's hand. "Today is a historic day for Mississippi." The press gathered around, cameras clicking. "Today, private enterprise is extending a hand to help government. Today, a great foundation has come to our state to start a great program for conservation."

I glanced at Pat. He was all smiles. The governor was spreading it on pretty thick.

"We are pleased," the governor continued, "that The Nature Conservancy and the St. Regis Paper Company have been able to work out a deal that will give Mississippi an opportunity to purchase a much-needed game and fish area on the Pearl River. We are honored that a representative of this great foundation has come to our state to see this property first hand. We hope that you will encourage the Conservancy to invest the first $3 million of your grant"—here the governor paused for effect—"the largest grant in the history of conservation, to help protect one of the finest natural areas left in all of Mississippi."

The reporters crowded in closer. The governor was doing great. Charlie had given him an excellent briefing. "And now," he concluded, "as a token of our appreciation, we would like to give you this gift for all you have done for conservation. We hope that each time you look at this little memento, you'll remember this day and your visit to the great state of Mississippi."

We all applauded dutifully as the governor handed Pat's package to the general counsel. The general counsel accepted the gift politely, but the governor's remarks obviously had not cracked his veneer.

The general counsel opened the package. Out came a belt with a brass buckle big as a fist, the kind only a real redneck would wear. The governor was visibly taken aback. Charlie Deaton nearly swallowed his cigar. The reporters pressed for a closer look. There was a collective gasp. Engraved on the buckle were the words "I Give Joy to Women." All heads swiveled toward the governor. The governor's head swiveled toward Pat.

"Obviously, you two must have met," Pat said impishly. The general counsel began to laugh. The governor began to laugh. Everybody began to laugh. The ice was broken.

We did the deal with St. Regis. The governor got the $3 million from the legislature. We rolled over the foundation's first installment into our next project. The Rivers of the Deep South program was becoming a reality.

As hoped, the foundation did carry conservation through the eighties. During that time, the trustees gave away over $100 million to thirty-two conservation organizations. Most of it, about $70 million, went to Conservancy projects. Through managing that money, I've gotten to know the general counsel. He remains calm, affable, and consistently polite on the surface, but still has a core of steel. After our trip to Mississippi, that no longer worries me. When things get too tight, I know how to loosen him up. I just suggest he unbuckle "I Give Joy to Women" a notch.

The 87th Day

THE GENERAL COUNSEL had such a good time in Mississippi that he wanted all of the trustees to see a project.

"I don't believe it," I said to Pat when he gave me the news. "How many rabbits do you think I have in my hat? We were lucky to pull out the Pearl River deal. I don't have an encore."

"You'd better find one," Pat told me. "The trustees want to see something this fall, just before they make their next distribution."

Distribution. He had said the magic word. If getting a grant from this foundation was difficult, performing on it was next to impossible. The trustees never just wrote a check for the full amount and said, best of luck. They stretched their grants out over time. They liked to make their distributions in December. That way, they could hold your feet to the fire while they collected more interest on their money.

Leverage and rollover. Leverage and rollover. That's all I ever heard from the trustees. Now that Watt had garrotted the federal land acquisition budget, I had to find a new source of funding.

If there were another rabbit anywhere in my hat, it had to be Florida. The state had just launched its Save Our Rivers program. The program was funded by an innovative transfer tax which the state levied on real estate. Five cents was added to the state's documentary stamp tax, so that the Save Our Rivers program got a nickel each time a hundred dollars' worth of real estate was sold. Five cents didn't sound like much, but an awful lot of property was sold in Florida. Income to the Save Our Rivers program over the first five years was projected to exceed $100 million. That money was divided between five newly created Water Management Districts.

In 1981, the Suwannee River watershed comprised the most rural section of Florida. Rising in southeast Georgia's Okefenokee Swamp, the river curls into Florida halfway between Jacksonville and Tallahassee. From there, it winds its way 263 miles south through north-central Florida, meeting the Gulf at Cedar Key. It was practically undeveloped. Much of the land around the river was owned by large timber companies like St. Regis, Continental Can, Buckeye, and Owens Illinois. We had good relations with all of these companies, many of whom were anxious to sell their slow-growing bottomland hardwoods and reinvest the proceeds into "supertrees," plantation pines that could be harvested after twenty years.

With the help of the timber companies, we already had protected both ends of the Suwannee River. The Union Camp Corporation had given us 16,000 acres in the Okefenokee Swamp, and we had worked a 50-percent bargain sale with Brunswick Pulp & Paper and Buckeye for another 15,000 acres on the Lower Suwannee National Wildlife Refuge. I was confident that we could buy more big blocks of land at bargain prices from the timber companies.

My plan was to pump new dollars into the Rivers of the Deep South program by convincing the Suwannee Water Management District to repurchase blocks of land that we would acquire along the river from the timber companies. The problem was that the Suwannee Water Management District had never heard of The Nature Conservancy. A Corp of Engineers mentality permeated all of the Water Management Districts. Their boards cared more about politics than conservation. Their staffs were made up of engineers who knew more about ditches and dams than flora and fauna. For over 200 years, engineers had been taught that waterways should be straight and clean and that wetlands should be filled and reclaimed. Reeducating them to think that natural systems might best be left alone was going to be a long, slow process.

The Suwannee District was the most contentious and parochial group of public officials that I had ever encountered. The board was a strange mixture of academics, timbermen, businessmen, farmers, and one school bus driver. They were like a pack of gators, a throwback to an earlier era. Everybody knew everybody, but nobody agreed with anybody. Board meetings often turned into genealogical debates over who said what to whom four generations ago. Outsiders were fresh meat when thrown in front of the board. As Don Morgan, the executive director, once told me after I had been chewed over, "We treat all our guests the same: crummy."

The Suwannee's board was skeptical of me and leery of my intentions. Who's this Yankee with a Boston accent telling us how to buy land? What is this Nature Conservancy? Where do they get their money? How do we know they aren't some Mafia front? And who is this big foundation that wants to save the Suwannee River? Even a Yankee foundation wouldn't put hard money into swamplands. Nobody's fallen for that scam in years.

The board was not agreeing to any deals until they knew us, and at their pace, that could take decades. I decided to use the old Mississippi trick. I'd have the trustees sell the board, and the board sell the trustees. It had worked before; maybe it would work again.

I arranged a trip along the lower Suwannee. One of the timber companies owned a nice bottomland hardwood tract just north of the

Suwannee National Wildlife Refuge. The company was willing to sell the land to the Conservancy for 70 percent of its fair market value. It would be a perfect kickoff project for the District.

I borrowed a plane from a friendly bank in Mobile. It was large enough so that we could pick up the four trustees in Atlanta, yet small enough so that we could land right at Cedar Key. I'd rent a boat at Cedar Key that would take us twenty miles up the river to the tract. There we would meet the board for a barbecue. We would spend the afternoon eating, drinking, touring the property, and getting to know one another. Afterwards, the trustees, Pat, and I would get back in the boat and cruise back down to Cedar Key, where I had booked rooms at a neat old inn. We'd have a nice dinner, discuss leverage and rollover, and be on our way bright and early the next morning.

Everything was looking good, except for the boat. Cedar Key was not Palm Beach; there were very few charters, and I knew that I couldn't dump the trustees into some old tub. I needed something nice. The best I could find was a 24-footer called *The 87th Day.* The boat was okay. The Captain wasn't.

He was a big blowhard, probably pushing sixty. He wore a thick gold chain with a gold medallion that looked suspiciously phallic. He had a Playboy bunny tattooed on his right forearm and wore a T-shirt that proclaimed, "Love Me or Leave Me." He'd just brought *The 87th Day* up from Key West. "Key West has gone to hell," he told me. "Ya can't tell the girls from the guys, not that it matters. Most of 'em bat lefthanded, if you get my drift." The word around Cedar Key was that the captain was running dope. This didn't bother me; that's what the locals said about everyone who came to Cedar Key, me included. What did bother me was the way the captain ran his mouth. He was bound to aggravate the trustees. They didn't like blowhards.

The bank's plane landed at Cedar Key right on time. The weather was perfect. It was a two-minute walk to *The 87th Day.* Its big diesels were purring as we came on board. The captain, who was slouched over the wheel, fiddling with the controls, stood up. "You boys are right on time. I thought you might stop for a little piece in Atlanta. Haw. Haw." I could see the trustees stiffen. They studied his tattoo and gold chain. They were not amused.

I quickly ushered them to the stern—as far from the captain as possible—as we chugged out of the harbor. The president, the treasurer, the secretary, and the general counsel seemed content to sit in their deck chairs, absorbing the scenery and the warm Florida sun. A great blue heron broke from a tree, swooped across the bow, and flapped upriver ahead of us, squawking our arrival, a standard-bearer for conservation. The president delighted in the water snakes basking in the branches along the bank. The treasurer chortled as a row of turtles looked up, hesitated, then plopped off a log, one by one, into the water. The secretary pointed excitedly as a family of mallards burst from the marsh. The general counsel trained his Leicas on a half-submerged log, sure that he'd spotted a gator.

The novelty of the river started to wear off after about ten miles. *The 87th Day* wasn't as fast as the captain had promised. It was getting hot, and the trustees were getting bored. Pat began to look edgy. "Would anybody care for something to drink?" I said. We all moved into the galley.

The galley of *The 87th Day* was a monument to Ernest Hemingway. A picture, in color, of the Sacred Heart of Jesus hung over one bunk. The Virgin of Cobre blessed the other. A copy of *The Old Man and the Sea* lay on the table. A faded photograph of Papa himself was mounted over the door to the head. It was signed, but the writing was illegible.

"What's that inscription on Hemingway's picture?" the treasurer asked the captain when he moved back on deck.

That was a mistake. Asking the captain a question was like lighting a fire under a hot-air balloon. He puffed himself up and said, "Oh, me'n Papa, we were old fishin' buddies. I was the guy who got'm his first marlin." I glanced at the president. His eyebrows raised. The president's father had founded the Foundation. The president had been trained since childhood to smell out phonies. He had just picked up the scent of something fishy.

"So you fished with Hemingway?" he asked.

"Oh yeah," the captain bragged. "Me'n Papa go back a long ways. He wrote that *Old Man and the Sea* right after I got'm his marlin." If the captain had just shut up then, the president might have ignored him. But he didn't. He puffed up even more. "He got all that stuff about fightin' the fish from me. I pract'ly wrote that book for'm."

"So the fish in *The Old Man and the Sea* is a blue marlin?" the president asked.

"Sure, had t'be. I got Papa that fish back in '50. Brought it right into Havana. Santiago, the old man, he was our deckhand. We was drunk for a week after we landed that one."

"You and Hemingway used to drink together?"

"All'a time," the captain said. "He knew I was the best fisherman in the Keys. He wouldn't go out with no one but me. We fished together, we drank together, even had a few women together."

This notion was so absurd that it left the president speechless. He turned away and walked to the stern. My worst fears were coming true. I wanted to tell the captain to shut up, but what do you say to some idiot who's just claimed to be Ernest Hemingway's fishing, drinking and philandering buddy?

We rounded a bend in the river, and there was the dock. A haze of smoke from the barbecue pit hung over a modest little hunting camp. The board of the Suwannee Water Management District approached the dock to greet us.

The barbecue couldn't have gone better. The trustees probed the board, and the board probed the trustees. By the end of the afternoon, they both liked what they saw. They agreed to go ahead with the deal. The Conservancy would buy the land from the timber company for 70 percent of its fair market value. We would finance the purchase with funds from the foundation's next distribution. Then we'd resell the land, at our cost, to the District when it had accumulated enough Save Our Rivers money. By purchasing this tract and leaving it in its natural state, the District would be committing itself to a policy of water management through natural area protection, the best-possible strategy.

I was euphoric. I skipped back to *The 87th Day.* A few drinks, a nice dinner, a good night's sleep, and we were home free.

Pat and I spent the return trip rehashing our meeting with the board and the details of the deal with the trustees. They liked the leverage. They liked the rollover. Thanks to the current, the trip downstream went much faster. We were back at Cedar Key ahead of time. While the captain pulled up to the dock, I briefed the trustees on the rest of our schedule. I had everything planned to the minute.

Then it happened. As he tied up to the dock and we prepared to get out, the captain started to pop off. "Too bad you boys are in such a hurry. Ya'll oughta slow down a bit. That's the trouble with Yankees, ya don't know how to enjoy y'selves. Y'always thinkin' bout some schedule when y'oughta be thinkin' about catchin' fish and chasin' women. Now, if ya'll stuck with me, ya'd have plenty of both."

I couldn't have cared less about catching fish or chasing women, especially with this blowhard. I just wanted to get the trustees out of there. I looked at the president. He was looking at the captain.

"You bigtime Yankees are so tight-assed, ya don't leave no time for fun. There's no sense comin' to the Gulf if ya don't know how to fish."

Little did the captain know that he had just delivered the ultimate insult. Not only had the president been trained to smell out phonies, he had been groomed as a world-class sportsman. He fished as easily as most people brush their teeth. The president calmly sighed like some professional gunfighter who had just been called out by a dumb sod-buster. He straightened up. "There ought to be some pretty good flats at the end of this river," he said.

I prayed that the captain had enough sense to shut up, but like all blowhards, he was too stupid. "Best in the world. This river spreads right out into a bed of grass."

"Should be good for specks and redfish."

"Catch 'em alla time," the captain boasted as he shut down the engines.

"Let's catch one now!" the president challenged.

"Ah, gee," I interrupted desperately. "It's time for cocktails. Remember the schedule. Don't you think we should settle in and get ready for dinner?"

"Nonsense," the president stated. "It will only take a few minutes. I don't want to fill the boat box. I just want to catch one fish. That shouldn't take too long, should it, Captain?"

"Well, I dunno," the captain hedged, obviously surprised at this turn of events. "It's kinda late, and the tide's runnin' out. Them fish don't bite good when the tide's goin' out."

"Surely Papa's old fishing buddy could find us just one fish," the president taunted.

I slumped down next to Pat as we chugged out of the harbor. Everyone threw in a line, but no one was getting so much as a nibble. The captain had a tackle box full of excuses. "They feed at night on a full moon." "That cold spell we had last week must have sent 'em south." "They don't bite when the tide's goin' out." He kept *The 87th Day* moving, searching for new grass beds. We were moving into really shallow water.

Thunk. We hit bottom just as the president got a bite. "Damn," said the captain.

The president reeled in a small speckled trout. "Well, what do you know," he said, holding up his fish. "Okay, Captain, let's head for home."

The captain revved up *The 87th Day*'s diesels, but we weren't going anywhere. We were stuck. I looked toward shore. There must have been two miles of water between us and Cedar Key.

"Seems like we're stuck," he groused, easing back on the throttles. "You boys'll have to jump over and try to push us free. That tide ain't gonna turn for a while yet, and we can't afford to lose no more water."

"You want us to jump overboard and push this thing home?" I asked incredulously.

"No, not all the way home," the captain scoffed. "Just till we find some water. It's either that, or spend the night." I looked at Pat. He was already stripping down. He was not about to spend the night.

Pat and I were both wearing our standard conservation-green Patagonia shorts. We jumped overboard. The water was just deep enough and cold enough to suit a soprano. We started pushing, and the captain revved the diesels. *The 87th Day* didn't budge.

Reluctantly, the secretary, treasurer, and general counsel began stripping down. Each was clad in white boxer shorts, undoubtedly Brooks Brothers. They plopped over the side, one by one, like turtles. As the captain revved the engines, mud and pieces of slimy eelgrass, chewed up by the props, spewed over us. The trustees looked like they had been mud wrestling. This had to be a low point for conservation.

"Push harder," the captain yelled. *The 87th Day* didn't budge.

"More help," we pleaded, wiping mud and grass from our eyes.

"You'd better get in there too," the captain told the president.

"You get in," the president said. "I'll drive."

"You can't drive *The 87th Day,"* the captain protested.

"The hell I can't!" the president said, seizing the throttles.

"What? I can't go overboard. I'm the captain."

"Not any more. Get in there and push while we still have some water," the president ordered. "We're not paying you to spend the night."

When the president told you to do something, you did it. Despite the mud, the grass, the cold, and the ignominy of our situation, we all started to laugh as the captain began to undress. A pair of skimpy red bikini shorts hinged his skinny white thighs to his bloated white belly. There was an ample bulge in the front of his shorts. Maybe he wasn't such a blowhard after all. He grumbled to himself as he lumbered over the side.

The president expertly began playing the throttles, rocking *The 87th Day* back and forth. On his signal we all gave a mighty hcavc. *The 87th Day* broke free. The president quickly found a channel and we scrambled to get back on board.

The captain couldn't make it. His skinny little arms couldn't hoist that big belly over the side. He clung to the rail thrashing his spaghetti legs. Pat picked up the gaff. "Here, grab this," he said, offering the round end to the captain.

Once the captain had hold of the hook, Pat braced his feet on the gunnel and pulled him in. The captain lay on the deck gasping, looking like a big fish out of water. His little red shorts had slipped down over his bottom, and bits of eelgrass clung to his head.

The president had *The 87th Day* almost to Cedar Key before the captain caught his breath, retired to the galley, changed his pants, and reclaimed the controls. He steamed into the harbor, this time with no talk of Yankees being too busy to enjoy life. This time the captain couldn't wait to get rid of us.

Pat regaled us at dinner with a recap of the mutiny. As a finale, he produced the captain's red bikini shorts, which he had somehow managed to swipe. He presented them to me. "Dave," he said, "given the success of the Rivers program, you just might be the man to fill these."

"Thank you, Pat," I said, accepting the shorts with exaggerated dignity. They were still wet and covered with mud and grass. I stuck my fist into the pouch, held them up and offered a toast. "Gentlemen. To the Rivers of the Deep South. May their support continue to swell."

I stole a look at the president. He was contemplating the captain's undies. "My goodness," he said. "That would be some endowment."

Doggone It

DOGS HAVE ALWAYS BEEN TROUBLE for The Nature Conservancy. They chase our fauna and defecate on our flora. Even worse, they ingratiate themselves with major donors. That's when they can really create problems. Competing with other nonprofits—the arts, education, medicine, and religion—is difficult, but we can do it. What we can't do is compete against some warm, cuddly, devoted bundle of affection that's won the heart of a potential patron.

Dogs are territorial. They can sense when someone else has designs on the hand that feeds them. They become very protective. They know when they've got a good deal, and they don't like other freeloaders mooching their Milkbones.

One of the classic Conservancy dog stories took place in 1976, when Pat Noonan was summoned south. A new state director needed help. For years this particular state program had been existing on a shoestring. Finally, the new director was on the threshold of a major breakthrough. She had identified a wealthy widow who could put the program permanently in the black and institutionalize The Nature Conservancy within her state.

The widow had agreed to host a dinner party for the Conservancy. The "who's who" of the state had been invited, and Pat was the guest of honor. All he had to do was sell the widow and her friends on the Conservancy.

No one was better at selling the Conservancy than Pat. He was the greatest fundraiser in conservation: quick on his feet, with just the right amount of irreverence. He borrowed my tux (I was the only member of the staff as stout as Pat), shined his shoes, and polished his speech. This dinner party had all the ingredients for success: good food, good drink, and a cornucopia of well-heeled donors. The affair was being held at the wealthy widow's home, an old plantation nestled along the banks of the Tennessee River. The guests were ferried from the parking lot up the magnolia-lined driveway by horse and carriage. They were greeted by a distinguished, gray-haired butler who ushered them across the portico and through the massive Doric columns to the living room. Pat was resplendent in my tux. All the guests were genuinely pleased to meet him. Only Calhoun seemed to resent his presence.

Calhoun was the widow's much-beloved Airedale. He was used to being the center of attention and didn't like the fuss the widow was making over Pat. He sat neglected in the corner as she bustled Pat around, chattering gaily about plants and wildlife. Pat could feel Calhoun's jealous glare all through cocktails, but what did he care? Calhoun didn't write the checks. Things were going so well that Pat, always the gracious victor, stooped to slip Calhoun an occasional pig in a blanket.

As the chimes sounded and the guests began to file into the dining room, Pat stood back politely with the widow. They would be the last to enter. Pat would seat the widow, and after grace, she would propose a toast to The Nature Conservancy. Pat would be asked to say a few words just before the soup. Nothing fancy, nothing formal. Just a friend talking to other friends about conservation.

As the last guest drifted to the table, Pat offered the widow his arm. She took it, smiled, and turned toward the dining room. It was then that Calhoun struck. He got Pat on the left buttock; it was a quick, piercing bite, clean and deep. Pat yelped and grabbed his behind.

He wheeled around. Calhoun was sitting there, happily wagging his tail. "Is something wrong?" the widow inquired.

Calhoun had him. Pat wanted to say, "Your goddamn dog just bit me in the ass," but, being the consummate professional, he caught himself. It was clear that if Pat accused Calhoun, it would embarrass the widow, and that would be it for the Conservancy.

Pat could feel the blood oozing into my trousers. "No, no," he said, re-offering his arm, "just a little cramp." Pat clenched his cheeks, swallowed his pride, and proceeded to give the speech that permanently endowed the state program. It was a landmark evening for the Conservancy. Not only had Pat saved a state office, he also set a new standard for dedication and personal sacrifice.

My own dog story is even more painful.

Apalachicola Bay is one of the most fertile estuarine systems in North America. It is formed where the Apalachicola River meets the Gulf of Mexico, about seventy miles southwest of Tallahassee. The Conservancy has been working for over twenty years to protect this estuary.

The bay is bounded by three barrier islands: St. Vincent to the west, St. George to the south, and Dog to the east. We were able to acquire all of St. Vincent in 1969 for a measly $1 million. Today, this 13,000-acre pristine barrier island is permanently protected as a national wildlife refuge.

St. George, the largest of the three islands, did not fare as well. Because it faces directly into the Gulf, the pounding surf has created thirty miles of pure, white sand beach. Developers are drawn to white sand beaches like ants to a picnic. They find them irresistible.

In the fifties, local entrepreneurs convinced the Florida legislature to authorize the construction of a toll bridge from the town of Apalachicola to St. George Island. Soon the beaches of St. George were being despoiled by ticky-tacky cottages. Now the state is spending millions on St. George to regulate development, to buy those areas which remain undeveloped, and to maintain an infrastructure of roads and utilities that are constantly being swept away by wind and wave.

Dog Island is the runt of the Apalachicola's litter, which may explain why it never achieved sainthood. Its 1,800 acres and three miles of "good" Gulf beach aren't worth a bridge, but still, Dog is big enough to accommodate a major development. More important, it is the only privately owned, relatively unspoiled island left in all of Florida.

There are many stories about how Dog Island got its name, but the one I like best goes back to when the French controlled the Gulf, during the late eighteenth century. They wanted to base their fleet in Apalachicola Bay, but the residents of Apalachicola and Carrabelle, the two towns on the mainland, wanted nothing to do with them. They assumed, correctly, that the sailors would deflower their daughters. They told the French admiral to "keep his dogs out on that island." Hence "Isle du Chien." Fearing a mutiny by his lusty crew, the admiral sailed on to Louisiana, where he and his men were well and often received by the less puritanical Cajun population.

"Isle du Chien," along with the rest of the estuary and the panhandle of Florida, was all but forgotten until after World War II. The whole area remained the domain of the St. Joe Paper Company. As late as 1950 the Florida panhandle was still mired in the 1800s. St.

Joe's workers were paid in company script, redeemable only at company stores, and logging crews were recruited from the state prisons. Prisoners were barged up the Apalachicola into the swamps to hand-cut the bottomland hardwoods, and rumor had it that many an unruly logger never made it back down.

Soon after the war, George Lewis, an ex-aviator and scion of the Lewis Bank of Tallahassee, bought Dog Island. George had no interest in banking and saw Dog Island as a perfect retreat for World War II pilots. Many of them would have trained at nearby Elgin Air Force Base and flown practice missions over Dog Island. George drew up plans for 1,500 cookie-cutter house lots, bulldozed a grass landing strip, set up a Quonset hut, installed a bar, and waited for his lost squadron to come flying home. It never happened. A few old warriors spied George's wind sock and dropped in, but as late as 1978 there were only eighty vacation homes and six permanent residences scattered across Dog Island's 1,800 acres. George came to like it that way. Everyone came to like it that way. People who found Dog Island were very individualistic, and in some cases, downright eccentric. They did not want Dog Island to be discovered, but they couldn't hide forever.

A big developer from Miami landed in 1978 and offered George $4 million. The developer was proposing a full-blown development, 1,500 units complete with swimming pools, tennis courts, and a golf course. George was tempted. A group of alarmed residents met with George and persuaded their old comrade to sell the island for conservation purposes for $2 million cash. They were aware of the Conservancy's ongoing interest in the estuarine system and gave us a call. Pat Noonan sent me to investigate.

At this time, the Conservancy was focusing its protection efforts on islands. Nevertheless, before the developer made his offer, we had little interest in Dog Island. It was already partially developed and, by itself, it didn't seem to be of any great ecological significance. It certainly was no Santa Cruz, but still Dr. Bob Jenkins, our head scientist, liked the idea of protecting what was left of the island as part of the Apalachicola estuarine system. Nobody liked the idea of paying $2 million. That was twice as much as we had paid for the much, much larger St. Vincent.

After visiting the island and looking at the data, I reported back to Pat that intensive development of Dog Island could pose a real threat to the entire estuarine system. I felt that we should purchase the island to protect our long-term investment in the estuary, provided that we could roll the money over, possibly by reselling the property to the state. A state park on Dog Island would serve two purposes. It would help protect the bay and offer the public a unique opportunity to visit an unspoiled barrier island. The state indicated that it was interested, and had the funding, provided that there was no opposition from the islanders. We polled the islanders. They said that they had no problem with a state park; in their eyes anything was better than a 1,500-unit intensive development. I recommended that we proceed.

Noonan was dubious. "Islanders are fickle," he warned. "They can't agree on anything. Once we own it, we'll be stuck."

"Don't worry, Pat," I assured him. "I'll personally handle this one." It was the dumbest statement I ever made.

Within a week the developer had sued for tortious interference with contract. This meant we couldn't close on the island. The case dragged on for two years. By the time we were ready to close, the state had redirected its funds to another project. I started looking for private funding. It became clear that, while foundations were glad to finance the protection of pristine barrier islands, they couldn't care less about ones which were partially developed. "Why create a private country club for the homeowners?" one said. "Let them pay for their own protection."

I went to the islanders. If I could raise enough from them, we might be able to lure the state back into the deal. A few were supportive; we raised $250,000. But this didn't even cover the interest on our loan, which had skyrocketed to 18 percent. As Pat had predicted, with the threat of development gone, most of the islanders were perfectly content to let the Conservancy own the land. Many now openly opposed the state park. Public ownership meant public access, and the islanders didn't want the townspeople from Apalachicola and Carrabelle coming over and deflowering their daughters.

In fact, they started badgering me to hire a manager. They wanted somebody to maintain security. We did need a manager. Junked cars and beer cans were starting to outnumber the flora and fauna. We advertised the position and heard from only one applicant, Dr. Lawrence Alexander.

Dr. Alexander, or just Alexander, as he preferred to be called, was one of the islander's six permanent residents. He claimed to have received a doctorate in General Studies from Emory University, and he professed to be a writer. When I met Alexander, he reminded me of a portly Indian chief. He was a big man, at least six-two, and easily tipped the scales at 250. His dark, shiny hair was tied in a ponytail and encircled by a red calico headband. Alexander was a self-taught biologist, and his knowledge of Dog Island's ecology seemed unlimited. I figured that this reclusive writer would be the perfect man for the job. When he wasn't working on his novel, he could tack up a few WARNING: NESTING AREA signs; and he was big enough to chase the kids and their all-terrain vehicles off the dunes. With Alexander as a manager, I would be free to spend all of my time scouring the country, looking for money.

After a few months, rumors began to float back from the island that Alexander was out of control, that he had gone mad with power. This heretofore reclusive writer was continually confronting the other islanders. He had closed off roads and denied people access to their property. He was waging war on a colony of raccoons that had invaded the island and were raiding the nests of our birds and turtles. Things really got out of hand when he started nailing raccoon carcasses to the trees. At last, all the islanders could agree on something: They despised Alexander.

I was too busy looking for support to check on him. Then I was presented with a potential major donor who had been referred to us by one of the Conservancy's founding fathers. Pat Noonan told me to call on her. "Get her interested in Dog Island," he admonished. As Pat had predicted, Dog Island had become our biggest problem.

The potential donor was another wealthy widow. We knew very little about her except that she lived on Park Avenue. After an encouraging phone conversation, I was invited to meet her at her apartment.

The yapping started as soon as I pressed the doorbell. It was coming from a toy poodle. It nipped at my ankles as the maid escorted me to the solarium. A large, heavy-set woman was occupying most of the sofa. The poodle leaped into her lap and was immediately smothered with hugs and kisses. His name was Pierre. I knew he was going to be trouble.

It is a well-known fact in fundraising that the more you talk, the less you get. Over tea, I listened and listened to try to determine the donor's interest in conservation. It soon became obvious that she knew nothing about biotic diversity. But that was not unusual; very few people knew anything about biotic diversity. She also didn't know much about the outdoors. She was a native New Yorker. To her, an outdoor adventure was a stroll along Fifth Avenue. It was Pierre who had sparked her interest in conservation. Since her husband's death, Pierre had become the focal point of her life. Pierre loved visiting the trees in Central Park.

"Dogs need more places to run," she declared.

"Say no more," I enthusiastically concurred. "Wait until you and Pierre see Dog Island."

"Dog Island?" she exclaimed. "That sounds delightful!"

The story about the French fleet seemed inappropriate. Instead, I described our work in Apalachicola Bay and stressed how the Conservancy was trying to create a "Central Park" for Dog Island. Could she help? She was interested. She accepted my invitation to visit the island two weeks later, which was the next full moon.

Whenever possible, the Conservancy likes to take potential donors to see preserves during a full moon. Nocturnal animals are visible; waterfowl are active and feeding; trees shine in a fantasy of silhouettes; ponds and streams shimmer in the moonlight. Along the coast, tides are drawn high, prompting marine life to come closer to shore. Plus, most people don't realize that a full moon rises in the east at precisely the same moment that the sun sets in the west. This lunar-solar exchange is one of nature's most impressive shows, staged once every twenty-eight days. The phenomenon was particularly effective on Dog Island where the Gulf forms both horizons.

Prudence dictated that I visit the island before the widow arrived. I wanted to check on Alexander, tour the preserve, and make sure that everything was set.

I was astounded when I saw Alexander. The portly chief had become a lean warrior. He was under two hundred pounds, and there was fire in his eyes. He told me that he had found his destiny, his essence, his purpose in life; it was to protect Dog Island. He no longer wasted time on his novel; instead, he was preparing a comprehensive inventory of the flora and fauna of Dog Island. He presented me with a first draft. "Start with this," he said proudly. "There's plenty more to come."

I could hardly lift it. It was over twelve hundred pages. "How could you lose all that weight, just from writing?" I asked incredulously.

"The only way to understand the preserve is to run it, every day."

"But that's over twenty miles!"

"So be it," replied Alexander.

I was not about to run anywhere, especially with the widow. Fortunately, I was able to borrow an old Packard touring car from one of our few remaining friends on the island. It would never make it on Park Avenue, but it was big, comfortable, and, after some work, clean. I was very impressed when I toured the island. Ecologically, Alexander had done an incredible job. He had fenced off all nesting areas, labeled hundreds of plants and trees, and tacked up NO TRESPASSING signs as far as the eye could see. Alexander might be as crazy as the loons that wintered on Dog Island, but so what. Our preserve looked great. The hell with the complaints; we weren't going to raise any more money from the islanders.

Now, all we had to do was make sure the widow was equally impressed. We rented the best available house on the Gulf side of the island, one with a screened porch where the widow could feel the cool breezes and watch the harvest moon rise over the beach. We spared no expense to provide a sampling of the local cuisine: world-famous Apalachicola oysters, Florida lobsters, shrimp, and snapper. We recruited islanders with pets who could make the case for a Central Park on Dog Island. Finally, I warned Alexander about Pierre. "Alexander, this is a nice elderly lady from New York City. She knows nothing about biotic diversity, and we can't expect to educate her overnight. Right now, her only interest in conservation is her dog. He likes Central Park. This dog is the most precious thing in her life. Whatever you do, don't say anything bad about it. They're only going to be here for one day. The important thing for now is to get her to like the island. The ecology can come later."

The day broke clear and calm. The plane I had chartered for the widow touched down on the grass strip right on time. We rolled the tourmobile out to meet her. Pierre came bounding out and made a beeline for some cattle egrets that were picking worms out of the runway. I could see a frown come over Alexander's lean, sunburned face. "Oh, isn't that cute," gushed the widow. "I can already see that Pierre likes Dog Island."

After a sumptuous lunch of shrimp and oysters, we started our tour. Pierre was in dog heaven. At each stop, he'd leap from the car and bark at the birds. The widow chortled with delight. It gave her great pleasure to see Pierre enjoy himself so thoroughly. Alexander's frown was tightening into a scowl. I could picture Pierre's carcass nailed to the nearest tree. "Take it easy," I whispered. "If you say a word, I'll strangle you." Then to the widow: "That Pierre is a real naturalist. He certainly knows his birds."

"Yes, this is a treat. All he gets to chase at home are pigeons."

Things got real tense when Pierre confronted a green turtle that was coming ashore. He yapped and yapped until it retreated into the surf. Pierre nipped at its tail as it reached the water. He pranced back to the widow, who was awfully amused. She didn't realize that the turtle was an endangered species. "Aren't you the brave boy," she praised. "You protected your mumma from that big old turtle." Alexander was in a silent rage. Somehow he managed to control himself.

I was tempted to say something. I was caught between Alexander's fanaticism and the widow's blissful ignorance. The pressure to get our money out of Dog Island and into other projects was affecting my judgment. If I'd told the widow that Pierre was harassing endangered species, she probably would have insisted that he be put on his leash. But it was too late now. The turtle was back in the water, and this was the end of the tour.

The reception and dinner that evening couldn't have gone better. The widow marvelled as the sun set and the full moon rose over the Gulf. The food was delicious, the guests polite and appropriately solicitous. As we said goodnight, the widow pulled me aside. "Pierre and I love Dog Island."

"It is a beautiful place," I agreed. "I hope that you can help us save it."

"I'm sure we can."

I could hardly believe it. The moonbeams dancing on the water reflected my glee. At last I had found some funding for Dog Island.

As the widow prepared to board her plane the next morning, she confirmed her commitment. I was ecstatic. I was paying no attention to Pierre. By now I had gotten used to his constant yapping. He had gone off for one last run at the cattle egrets. Tomorrow he'd be back chasing pigeons in Central Park.

Alexander and I were about to hoist the widow into the plane when she called for Pierre. We were all surprised to see him down by the water. He was yapping furiously at something in the lagoon. I saw two eyes glaring back at him. Probably another turtle, I figured. Then I looked at Alexander. For the first time in two days, he was smiling.

I quickly looked back at Pierre. A scream caught in my throat as the lagoon came alive. There was a mighty splash as a full-grown gator erupted from the water. For the first time in two days, Pierre was silent. He was paralyzed with fear. The widow shrieked and went limp in my arms. My knees buckled, but her shriek mobilized Pierre. He turned and took off down the beach.

Few people realize how fast a gator can cover 40 yards, especially when chasing a delicacy like Pierre. Pierre's coiffured little legs were churning like a Waring blender. Still, it looked bad. The gator was gaining. "Wow," observed Alexander, "look at them go. Those gators sure do love little dogs." I got the distinct impression that Alexander was rooting for the gator. The widow had revived and was bellowing, "Oh, Pierre, my Pierre. Run, baby, run!" Just as the gator opened his jaws to snap up Pierre, Pierre cut sharply back toward us. He was coming home to mumma.

Gators aren't built for lateral movement. The jaws slammed shut, but Pierre wasn't there. The gator was left with a snoutful of sand. Pierre had escaped. He nearly knocked the widow over as he leapt into her waiting arms. Tears were streaming down her face.

What could I do? I tried to make light of the incident. "Boy, that sure was exciting. Old Pierre almost bit off more than he could chew. Ha. Ha." The widow saw no humor in the situation.

"Exciting? You think that was exciting? That was horrible. I almost lost my Pierre." Now she was getting angry. "He should have been on his leash. Why didn't you warn me? Why did you let him run wild? This place is a jungle." With that, still clutching Pierre to her bosom, she attempted to get into the plane. When I tried to take her arm, she turned and glared at me. "No, thank you." She flopped through the door and ordered the pilot to take off.

Just the other day, I bumped into Pat Noonan. He hasn't been president of the Conservancy for eight years now. "How are you coming with Dog Island?" he inquired impishly. Everyone knows that I'm still having trouble with it. Dogs have always been trouble for The Nature Conservancy.

The Big Bust

BY THE FALL OF 1982, it was obvious that we were in big trouble on Dog Island. Thanks to the cutbacks in federal funding for land acquisition, the Conservancy was having financial problems with a lot of its projects: All of our permanent capital was tied up in land and we had very little money for new projects. It was becoming critical to get our money out of Dog Island.

I consulted with Pat Noonan. "Pat," I said, "do you think the trustees would have any interest in Dog Island?"

"Hmm. No leverage. No rollover." That didn't sound good. "But they *are* interested in barrier islands. It might not hurt to ask."

I was surprised when the trustees accepted our invitation to visit Dog Island. When was a good time? I quickly consulted my lunar calendar. "How about October 25th?" I suggested.

"Perfect, but on one condition," replied the president. "We *must* be back on the 26th for a dinner with Joe Paterno. We like Joe."

"No problem!" I said wittily. "The Conservancy always roots for the Penn State Nittany Lions." The trustees nodded their approval.

Again, I borrowed a plane from our friends at the bank in Mobile so we could pick up the trustees in Atlanta. Again, I rented the best house on the Gulf so the trustees could feel the cool breezes and watch the full moon rise over the water. Again, I spared no expense to provide a sampling of the local cuisine. Finally, for dinner, I recruited islanders who were businessmen, good Republicans who knew the virtues of free enterprise. We were set.

The bank's plane touched down on the grass strip right on time. It was a perfect day, warm and sunny, with a gentle breeze blowing off the Gulf. The clear blue October sky made the sand whiter than I had ever seen it. The island never looked better. The weather was so nice that the trustees impetuously decided to go for a swim in the Gulf. Pat was amazed to see these typically staid and proper businessmen frolicking like schoolboys in the surf. I had a tough time persuading them to break for lunch. We ate informally on the porch. The trustees dove into a huge platter of fresh shrimp and oysters. A group of porpoises found a school of fish right in front of us. They were joined by a flock of pelicans and a lone osprey. We all feasted on the bounty from the Gulf.

An afternoon tour of the island was equally fulfilling. Pintails and mallards, early arrivals from the Central Flyway, jumped from the marshes. We almost ran over a big king snake that was basking in the sun on the warm, sandy road. The island seemed to be doing everything it could to sell itself.

The dinner and reception that evening couldn't have gone better. We all marveled as the sun set and the full moon rose over the Gulf. The locals were charming, appropriately gracious, and refreshingly Republican. Old George Lewis dropped in to swap war stories with the trustees. We all were amazed when George, after a few belts, claimed that the *Enola Gay* prepared for its attack on Hiroshima by flying practice missions over Dog Island. "Were it not for Dog Island," he claimed, "we never would have won the war." We all enthusiastically agreed. As we said goodnight, the president pulled Pat and me aside. "Thanks for a great day," he said generously. "This place is all right. Do you know what I mean?"

We nodded knowingly.

The next morning, after a long walk on the beach and a refreshing dip in the Gulf, we were set to leave. When we got to the airstrip, we encountered our first problem. It had gotten hot, and the pilot didn't want to take all six of us off the island at once. "Hot air is thinner than cold air," he explained, "so we don't get as much lift. This grass runway is barely within specs. We have plenty of time, so why push it? There's a macadam strip just across the bay in Carrabelle. It's out in the middle of nowhere, but it's only a five-minute trip. I'll ferry you over in two groups."

"Fine," I said. "In fact, why don't the trustees go first. You can give them a tour of the Bay. Go out a few miles and come in real low, so they can see the other islands and get a feel for the estuarine system."

Pat and I retired to the shade of the Quonset hut as the trustees took off. Old George Lewis was sitting there by himself, listening to his ship-to-shore radio. George looked as though his stories had gotten the better of him; he was not in a talkative mood. Pat and I were so pleased with ourselves for having found some funding for Dog Island that we hardly noticed the intermittent squawks from the radio. We were surprised when George suddenly came to life. "I think you boys might have a problem," he said, pointing toward the radio.

Someone with a heavy drawl sounded very excited. "Yes sirree, them boys are lookin for a place to land." Squawk. "This must be the drop we heard about. Ovah."

Someone else, equally excited, responded. "Sheriff, they ain't landin heah. They musta seen us. They're headin for Carrabelle. Ovuh."

"We hear 'em, Cecil." Squawk. "They're comin' our way. Get on over heah on the double. We'll need some backup. Ovuh."

"Load 'em up, Sheriff. That's one fancy plane. Them boys might be packin Uzis. Ovuh."

"Waal. If they lookin' for trouble, we'll Uzi them right into a pine box. Ovuh."

I looked at Pat. "It's probably not the trustees," I said optimistically.

"Don't bet on it," Pat said with a frown.

I turned to George Lewis. "George! Get on the radio! Tell those guys they've made a mistake!" I said, now becoming frantic.

"Can't," said George. "That's police band. This is a marine radio. We can monitor, but we can't transmit."

Squawk. "They jus landed! Hail, Cecil, he ain't even turnin off the motor. That boy wants out."

"Hang on, Sheriff! We jus' passin' the Po' Boy."

"Wall, don't you stop for nuthin' to eat!" Squawk. "Four of 'em jus got out, and they look mean."

I stood up. I pleaded with George. "Can't you do anything?"

A thought clearly crossed George's mind. "Where's all those boys' money come from, anyway? They ain't running drugs, are they?"

I sunk back into my chair. "Pat, think of something!"

"I hope the Sheriff's a Republican," was all Pat said.

At that moment we heard our plane returning. Pat and I sprinted out and piled on board. The pilot had no idea of what was happening. He had taken off before the police arrived. As we landed in Carrabelle, we could see the trustees spread-eagled over a couple of police cruisers. One group of officers was holding them at gunpoint; others were dumping their luggage onto the runway. When we pulled up, a bullhorn told us to "cut the engine and get out with your hands on top of your heads."

They proceeded to search the plane, our luggage and even us. The trustees were visibly upset. It took me more than an hour to convince the Sheriff, the Highway Patrol, the Marine Patrol, and a member of the state's Drug Enforcement Agency that we were not drug-smugglers from Jamaica but conservationists from Dog Island. The Sheriff was visibly disappointed. He thought for sure he'd just made the big bust. Cecil told him to cheer up, he'd treat him to a Po' Boy.

By the time we got to Atlanta, the trustees had missed their connection. There would be no dinner with the pride of the Nittany Lions, and no grant for Dog Island. When they finally took off, the president said, "I think we've seen enough of Apalachicola Bay."

As Pat and I sat in the Crown Room at Hartsfield International Airport having a few belts, we watched the sun setting behind the runway. We didn't bother to look back. We knew it would be many moons before we found some funding for Dog Island.

Kansas City

DURING THE MID-SEVENTIES, I was doing a lot of projects in the Southeast. Most of my flying was done on Delta. That meant I had to go through Atlanta. I would buy a coach ticket (everyone in the Conservancy always flew coach), and reserve seat 21A, the window seat next to the emergency exit, which gave me four extra inches of legroom, and the seat in front of me had to be kept in the upright position at all times. I'd gratefully accept my rubber chicken and politely try to persuade the person in 21B to become a member of the Conservancy. I was a poor, humble conservationist.

Then Jimmy Carter got himself elected president of the United States. Travelling on Delta through Atlanta became impossible. Every flight was overbooked, reservations had to be made weeks in advance. Even then, young, arrogant Dixicrats, most of whom looked like Hamilton Jordan, were always trying to bump you. A poor, humble conservationist couldn't do his business this way. When the donor calls, you have to answer. You can't risk being left at the gate.

I ended up spending a lot of time sitting in Hartsfield International. During one interminable wait, I wandered over to see what

Eastern was doing. Frank Borman was trying to launch the "Wings of Man" but wasn't having much luck. Eastern still had a terrible reputation. They gleefully honored my Delta ticket and put me right on board, seat 21A. It was an easy flight, and soon I was flying Eastern as much as Delta.

By the time Jimmy Carter was bumped back to Plains, Eastern had made Atlanta one of its hub cities, and the Conservancy had begun its Rivers of the Deep South program. I hired Dick Ludington as the project coordinator for Rivers of the Deep South. Dick was a bright UNC graduate who loved to get a deal. He worked out of Chapel Hill; when we traveled together, we'd meet in Atlanta.

One day in the spring of 1981, we were both booked to Tallahassee on Eastern. When we checked in at Hartsfield, Dick presented the Eastern agent with a card. It said "Executive Traveler." Dick was immediately ushered to first class. I was stuck in coach next to a fat lady with two screaming kids. As soon as we were airborne, Dick sent me back a drink with a note that said, "Dave, when you get a card, come join me."

I was determined to have one of those cards. The minute I got home, I called the head of customer relations at Eastern's Washington office. "I want one of those cards," I told her.

"Sorry, we're overcommitted," she said. "But I'll be happy to put you on the list."

I called my travel agent. "Send a copy of my bookings to Eastern," I demanded. "And add a note, 'He wants his card NOW.' " At that time, I was the agency's number-one traveler. The very next day, I received a registered letter from Eastern. Inside was my Executive Traveler card, my ticket to first class. From then on, I flew exclusively Eastern, seat 1A. I loved going first-class; free drinks, good food, lots of room, quiet, courteous service. I no longer felt like a poor, humble conservationist; I felt like a captain of industry. When the person in seat 1B asked me what I did, I'd say, "I'm in real estate." I never mentioned the Conservancy.

In the mid-eighties, thanks to a $25-million grant from the same foundation that funded the Rivers of the Deep South, we initiated our National Wetlands Program. One of the first projects under this program was in California. That meant I would have to start flying west. I checked the flights. Eastern had the best fares, but their flights weren't direct. They all connected through Eastern's new hub in Kansas City.

I bought a coach ticket, but didn't bother to reserve seat 21A. I was going first-class. I checked in, flashed my card, and watched in horror as the agent shook her head. "Sorry, Mr. Morine, it doesn't look good. The Kansas City flight is completely booked. At most we might have one upgrade to first class."

"Booked? Hmm. All right, give me seat 21A, and please try to get me the upgrade."

She punched some buttons. "Sorry, 21A is not available. All we have are center seats."

"What!? You've gotta be kidding. You're going to make me spend six hours in a center seat?" I looked around at the herd lowing in the lounge. "Surely you can move somebody. I'm an Executive Traveler!"

"I'm sorry, Mr. Morine," the agent said. "You should have reserved your seat when you bought your ticket. I'll give you 16B and call you just before boarding if you can upgrade." She punched some more buttons. "Be sure to get in line early in Kansas City. Right now there's only three seats available in first class on the flight to San Francisco."

The cattle started milling around the gate. There was a delay in boarding. Some guy needing special assistance was making a big stink. He was confined to a fancy electric wheelchair, which he insisted on bringing into the cabin. The flight attendant said that he would have to check it, that it wouldn't fit in coach. "Then move me up to first class," he demanded.

Fat chance, I thought. There's only one seat left in first class, and it's gonna be mine. I'm an Executive Traveler.

"You've got the cheapest excursion fare," the flight attendant said, studying his ticket. "Are you willing to pay for an upgrade?"

"No way," the guy in the wheelchair shouted. "I'm an attorney with the Association for Handicapped People. We have an agreement with all the airlines that says you have to take my chair into the cabin."

Agreement? I thought. Who's this guy kidding?

The flight attendant looked at her watch, walked over to consult with the agent, came back, and wheeled the guy on board.

I raced to the desk. "What about my upgrade?"

"Sorry, Mr. Morine. First class is totally full."

When I got on the plane, the wheelchair was stowed in the galley and the guy was reclining in seat 1A, sipping what should have been my free drink. I struggled back to seat 16B.

I contemptuously rejected my rubber chicken and refused to acknowledge the two heifers on either side of me. In my mind, I was already ensconced in seat 1A, dining on filet mignon and sipping a fine California Cabernet as we passed over the Rockies. I was going to be the first person upgraded in Kansas City.

When the plane touched down, I checked my watch. We were twenty minutes late. That was not going to help my chances of upgrading. I stood up while we were still taxiing and clambered over the poor woman next to me. I ripped my bag from the overhead compartment, paying no heed to the blankets, pillows and coats that came tumbling down with it. I ignored the flight attendant's instructions to "remain seated with seatbelts securely fastened until we are at the gate" and staggered up the aisle. I made my way past seat 1A to the door. The handicapped guy eyed me suspiciously. "I want to be the first one off," he said to the flight attendant. "We're late, and I'll need the extra time to get upgraded to San Francisco."

Ha, I thought. That chair's gonna need rockets to beat me. "You'll have to wait until the other passengers have disembarked," the flight attendant told him. "Your Association has no agreement about deplaning." I grinned maliciously. This guy had outsmarted me in Washington, but now I had him.

The door opened and I broke for the gate. When I hit the terminal, I noticed a men's room. I looked over my shoulder. I had a healthy lead on the rest of the herd, and the wheelchair was nowhere in sight. I figured I had time to take a pee.

I ducked into the men's room and stepped up to the first urinal. I gave my bladder an impatient squeeze, but in my haste it was too hard. I quickly clenched my cheeks, praying I hadn't fudged my undies.

I waddled toward the nearest stall. The rest room was filling up. Our whole flight was catching up with me. The first stall was occupied. Still squeezing my cheeks, I shuffled to the second. It too was occupied. People were streaming past me. They quickly claimed the third, fourth, fifth, and sixth. Finally, the only stall left was the handicapped. The door was ajar. I went in, locked it, and busily began rehabilitating my undies.

I was almost done when I heard the whir of a motor coming my way. I saw a pair of wheels pull up to the door. I froze. There was a banging on the door. "Handicapped," a voice said. It was the same voice that had beaten me out of seat 1A. This guy obviously knew his rights. If he caught me in the handicapped stall, he'd probably have me arrested.

"Handicapped," I lied. There was another whir. The wheels retreated. I quickly finished my paperwork, made myself presentable, picked up my bag, unlocked the door, threw my coat over my head and hurried past the wheelchair.

"Hey! You're not handicapped! Somebody grab him!" he yelled. Everybody turned their heads, but fortunately nobody had a free hand.

I looked like O.J. sprinting through the terminal. Despite my little mishap, I was still one of the first in line. "I want to be as far back in coach as possible," I instructed the agent, pushing my Executive Traveler card deep into my pocket.

"All we have left are center seats in smoking."

I heard a familiar whir. "That's fine. Can I go right on?"

My eyes were watering by the time we got to San Francisco. My clothes smelled like they had spent the day at the Smokehouse Cafe. I was trapped between a guy who made stereos for tractor cabs and a salesman for Hallmark Cards. They both wore leisure suits and were chainsmokers. They had little interest in conservation. It didn't matter. I was back in coach where I belonged, trying to sell the Conservancy.

The next to last passenger off the plane was the guy in the wheelchair. The last was a contrite conservationist with slightly fudged undies.

Mother Nature

BIL GILBERT IS A GREAT OUTDOORSMAN and the writer the *Washington Post* has called "our best full-time environmental journalist." Bil has come up with an interesting theory.

"Up until the fifties," he told me over breakfast the other day, "just about everyone was scared to death of Mother Nature. They thought she was some mean old bitch who delighted in floods, fires, droughts, and swarms of locusts. She was something right out of the Old Testament. Most people wanted to be saved from her. They wanted to live in urban environments where Mother Nature could be controlled with things like air conditioning and DDT.

"Today," Bil continued, "all that has changed. Mother Nature has turned into some anorexic young waif that is slowly dying before our eyes. People want to protect her, embrace her, and save her for future generations. The public's perception of Mother Nature has completely changed."

"Why's that?" I asked.

"Simple," he said, taking a long drag on the butt that's always hanging from his mouth. "They want to go back to the fifties, when the cities were livable environments, when roads weren't continually clogged, when you could take a ride in the country and see cows instead of shopping centers. They're more afraid of cars and crime than they are of locusts and bears.

"Most environmentalists don't know anything about the real Mother Nature. That's all right, if you admit it. What gets me are all these holier-than-thou types that are always whining about the environment while what they're really doing is just trying to protect their own lifestyles."

I winced. More than one person has linked my interest in conservation with my secret desire to recapture the fifties. I was raised in a nice suburban environment. My family adhered to very strong middle-class values. The closest I came to meeting Mother Nature was the two weeks we spent in Maine every summer. Jordan's Camps were rustic, but they were a long way from wilderness.

I fit very nicely into Bil's theory. I never knew the real Mother Nature. Bil sees my brand of conservation as a form of nostalgia. The worse the cities get, the more I want to get back to Jordan's Camps. And, according to Bil, most conservationists are a lot like me. When they were kids they went to camp, or to the shore, and had a great time. To them, Mother Nature is the young, anorexic waif. They've never met that mean bitch from the Old Testament.

I met her once. We were introduced by a friend of mine named Skipper Tonsmeire. He lives in Fairhope, Alabama, right on Mobile Bay. Skipper makes his living as a developer, but spends most of his time working in conservation. Skipper was the primary force behind The Nature Conservancy's efforts to save large sections of the Mobile/Tensaw Delta, Mobile Bay, and Alabama's Gulf Coast. He has done more for conservation in Alabama than just about anyone.

Skipper enjoys flirting with Mother Nature. It's not my young waif that he courts, but Bil Gilbert's mean bitch. He, like Bil, is a real outdoorsman. It bothers him that I am content to spend my time sitting in an office doing deals rather than trudging through the wilds. When I visit Skipper, he tries to toughen me up. He makes me sleep on the floor and dive into the bay before breakfast.

Skipper loves to run rivers. Every fall, he and his four younger brothers organize a float. Inevitably, a couple of brothers can't make it. That's when friends get invited. My turn came in 1980. The river was the Tatshenshini, one of the most remote rivers in North America.

According to my map, the Tatshenshini starts somewhere in the Yukon, runs southwest through British Columbia, and eventually empties into southeast Alaska's Dry Bay. I had no desire to see any of these places. I very politely said no, that I was busy, that I was working on a big deal, that I didn't have any time, that they should find somebody else. Skipper would not take no for an answer. I was going to float the Tatshenshini; I was going to experience the wilderness.

The group that met in Juneau on September 10, consisted of Skipper, his brother Pepper, Skipper's friend Pat Ogburn from Mobile, me, and a Canadian named Loch McSomething. I never did catch Loch's last name, not that it mattered. Where we were going, I'd have no occasion to introduce him to anyone. I did learn that he ran a dive boat in the Grand Caymans. That was how Skipper knew him. Skipper dives off of Grand Cayman.

After an all-night ferry ride to Haines and a three-hour drive over a single-lane dirt road into the Yukon Territory, we stopped. I figured our driver needed to take a leak. I didn't see any river. I didn't see anything; we were on a desolate, featureless, windswept plain out in the middle of nowhere. I began to wish that I was back in my office. "How much further do we have to go?" I asked.

"We're here," said Pepper. "Start unloading."

"Here" was Dalton Post, a long-abandoned hunting station at the confluence of the Klukshu and Tatshenshini rivers. I was disappointed. I had expected Dalton Post to be some quaint frontier town with a general store and a log saloon, the kind that Sergeant Preston used to frequent for a sarsaparilla. Right then, in fact, I was hoping for something a little stronger than a sarsaparilla. I grabbed my duffle and walked down the bank. Even with help from the Klukshu, the Tatshenshini didn't look like much of a river. At this point, she was just a glacial stream. I couldn't see why she would be of much interest to anyone as experienced as the Tonsmeires. "This is it?" I asked.

"Don't worry," Pepper assured me, "she'll give you a thrill before it's over."

After unloading, we inflated two rubber rafts: a big one that held four people comfortably and a smaller one that could be rowed by one person and was used to carry most of the gear. We pushed off. Skipper manned the little raft, while Pepper, Pat, Loch, and I followed. The Tonsmeires felt obligated to split up. That way, one could look after the guests while the other took care of the equipment.

Over the next few days, the Tatshenshini picked up strength. She left the plain and wound her way through the rugged St. Elias range. We passed Mount Fairweather, the highest peak in Canada. On the fourth day, we came out of the mountains into a valley. We had been treated to an exceptional morning, clear, hot, and sunny. Quaking aspen and yellow birch were shimmering in the sunlight. We all had our shirts off. Skipper even went for a swim before lunch. I put my toe in. It immediately went numb.

The valley was about four miles wide and eight miles long. Pepper, who had floated the Tatshenshini before, mentioned during lunch that we would camp at the bottom of the valley. It would be our last night on the Tatshenshini. When she emerged from the valley, she would be absorbed by the much larger Alsek. It was the Alsek that would take us to Dry Bay, 175 miles northwest of Juneau.

Eight miles didn't seem like much of a run. "How come we're not going all the way to the Alsek?" I asked.

Pepper gave me a knowing look. "You want to be fresh when you leave the Tat. She don't let go easily."

The sun felt good as we cleaned up after lunch. The Tatshenshini looked smooth and serene as she prepared for her meeting with the Alsek. I volunteered to row the little raft for the afternoon. That would give Skipper a chance to be with his brother and friends, and it would give me a chance to get away from Loch. Loch was getting on my nerves. He talked incessantly and, like many Canadians, was openly critical of America. According to Loch, Ford was an idiot, Carter was a stupid peanut farmer, Reagan was a washed-up actor, and America was responsible for all of the world's problems. If that wasn't enough, Loch inevitably lit up a joint after lunch. Sober, Loch was annoying; wrecked, he was intolerable. What I needed was a quiet afternoon by myself, a chance to view the wilderness without having to squint through a blue cloud of marijuana. The little raft would be a welcome escape.

I was still shirtless when we pushed off. Skipper threw me my shirt, vest, and raingear. "Keep these with you," he said. "They might come in handy." I couldn't see why. There wasn't a cloud in sight except for the one hanging around Loch.

We drifted peacefully along for about a mile. I lay back on the oars and soaked up the wilderness. It was very enjoyable. No phones, no pressure, nobody telling me I had to do something. Maybe Skipper was right. Maybe I should spend more time in the wilds.

Soon I was preoccupied with thousands of Canada geese milling around overhead, waiting for a front that would take them south. I marveled at their lack of symmetry. There were no neat V's or obvious leaders, just total bedlam. This prelude to their fabled migration looked and sounded like an Italian traffic jam.

Through the honking, I heard a shout. "Over here! Pull over here!"

I swiveled in my seat. The Tatshenshini was breaking up. The main channel and the big raft were going to the right. I was going to the left. I leaned into the oars with everything I had, but it was too late. Pepper smiled and gave me a little wave goodbye. "See you later," yelled Loch as he sat there puffing away. Within seconds, the big raft floated behind a line of trees. I was alone in the wilderness.

No big deal, I thought. We're probably just going around an island. Pepper knew the river. If there were any problems, he would have told me to pull over. The Tatshenshini had to come back together sooner or later. All I had to do was keep floating.

I reached for my shirt. It was getting cold. The sky was suddenly overcast. A front was coming through. I looked up at the geese. The traffic jam was beginning to unsnarl. Familiar V's started to form as the leaders caught the wind. Singles were flying from group to group, attempting to link up with the right flock. I could sympathize with their plight.

A cloud bank descended into the valley. Soon it was raining, lightly at first, then much harder. The temperature must have plummeted by thirty degrees. I was thankful to have my vest and raingear.

It became evident that we were not going around an island. The Tatshenshini kept braiding into smaller and smaller strands. I kept bearing to the right, toward the big raft and my only contact with civilization. I should have followed the main current, because my channel soon dwindled to a trickle.

I got out, grabbed the rope, and began to pull the raft over the gravel. It made a terrible grinding noise. I was afraid that I would puncture the skin. Then what would I do?

I had left my waders in the big raft. My boots were soaked, my feet were cold. My glasses were useless; the rain and my own panting kept them permanently fogged. I had to take them off to see anything, and everything I saw looked like a blurred grizzly. Now I was getting nervous. Two weeks in Maine every summer had not prepared me for this introduction to the real Mother Nature.

I had no idea of the time or how long I had been separated. The Tonsmeires didn't allow any watches on their trips; to them, watches signified appointments, commitments, schedules, all the things I was used to. The Arctic day was still fourteen hours long, so I had plenty of light, but I was getting tired. Slogging through the gravel pulling the raft was taking a toll. My feet were going numb, and my hands were ripped and raw from the rope. Of course, I had no gloves; they too were in the big raft.

Between the rain and my sweat, I was drenched to the skin. I was starting to shiver. I tried to remember what I had read about hypothermia. What would happen if I passed out? I thought about stopping and trying to make a fire, but how would I make a fire when everything was wet? And what would the others do? I had most of the gear. I had to keep going.

Sometime, much later, the rain stopped. I cleared my glasses and was relieved to see that the valley was narrowing. The raft offered less resistance as the water rose against my boots. I flopped back in and tried to row, but my hands had no feeling. I lay back and shoved them down into my groin.

I must have dozed off for a while. When I looked up, I had reached the bottom of the valley. I became euphoric. I had met Mother Nature head on. I had conquered the wilderness. Triumphantly I glided around the final curve. The raft picked up speed. The Tatshenshini was suddenly swollen from the rain. Ahead lay a gorge. I heard a familiar roar. It reminded me of the Great Falls of the Potomac, the falls that kill an average of eight people a year. I recalled Pepper saying that we wanted to be fresh when we left the Tat. Now I understood why. He knew her intimately. He knew that we needed all of our strength for this last encounter.

I spotted the big raft bobbing in an eddy that formed where the Tatshenshini's two limbs reunited. Skipper was standing in the raft, waving me over. I strained at the oars. I had to get into the vortex before the Tatshenshini came together for her final plunge into the gorge.

I wasn't going to make it. I was going to miss Skipper by a couple of yards. "Throw the rope! Throw the rope!" he yelled. I fumbled in the icy water sloshing in the bottom of the raft. By the time I found the rope, it was too late. I was past him. Skipper was shouting instructions. "Tie down the equipment! Keep your bow downstream! Don't get turned around! We'll be right behind you!" I could tell by the look on his face and the urgency in his voice that I was in trouble.

The little raft was swept into the gorge. I frantically looked for a place to land. A cliff of blue ice was on one side, solid rock on the other. Giant waves spumed over me. I became frozen with fear. I thought of my wife and young son. Would I ever see them again? I let go of the oars and hugged the seat. The raft twisted and bent as we hurdled through the rapids. I was sure I was going to be cast into the Tatshenshini. If she got me, she'd never let me go.

It was over in a matter of seconds. I came into the Alsek. I watched as the gray-green Tatshenshini reluctantly gave herself over to her brown, muddy companion. The big raft pulled up next to me. They were all exhilarated. I was still shaking.

I've never been back to Alaska. The next summer, I built a rustic little cabin on Kezar Lake in Maine. For two weeks every summer that's where I go to try to recapture the fifties. When Skipper calls, I tell him to "come on up. We've got an extra bunk, and there's plenty of hot water." He came only once, and didn't stay long. Too many people, too much noise, too boring.

I'm afraid to invite Bil Gilbert. If he were to come, it would only confirm his theory. I am too wedded to soft beds and hot showers to get intimate with the real Mother Nature. I want nothing to do with that mean bitch of the Old Testament. I'm perfectly comfortable in the fifties.

A Rising Tide

THE NATURE CONSERVANCY'S Virginia Coast Reserve, or "VCR" as it is commonly known, is the Conservancy's greatest assembly. It encompasses fourteen of the eighteen barrier islands that parallel the Virginia eastern shore, contains over 40,000 acres, and runs for more than sixty miles. It is the longest stretch of natural beach left on the Atlantic coast.

Pat Noonan created this reserve. He's been working on it for twenty years, first as the Conservancy's director of operations, then as president, and finally, as a consultant. Pat started the VCR back in the early 1970s, when a developer proposed turning the three southernmost islands—Shipshoal, Myrtle, and Smith—into the next Ocean City.

Virginia, for all its coastline, has very little accessible beach. By 1970, this lack of accessible public beach elsewhere in the commonwealth was putting tremendous pressure on Virginia Beach, the one stretch of Virginia coastline that can be reached by state road. Overcrowding was becoming chronic. The only logical escape was across the Chesapeake Bay Bridge Tunnel to the Eastern Shore.

The problem for beachgoers was that after they paid the $9.00 toll to cross the Bay Bridge Tunnel, there was no place to go. The entire sixty miles of the Eastern Shore is fronted by one giant marsh. The beaches are out on the barrier islands, and they can be reached only by private boat.

The developer was petitioning the Virginia Assembly to build a bridge across Cape Charles, the southernmost tip of the Delmarva Peninsula, to Smith Island, then run a road through the marsh to Myrtle and Shipshoal. "From there," the developer told the assembly, "the commonwealth could keep pushing the road north until it eventually connected all eighteen islands."

He stressed that this plan would open up miles of "wasted" beach to the public and bring great prosperity to the Eastern Shore. The assembly liked the idea. For years, the politicians in Richmond had been trying to figure out what to do with the Eastern Shore. Now they had an answer. Any good politician could see that more public beaches meant more tourists, which meant more prosperity, which meant more votes.

Biologists familiar with the ecology of the Eastern Shore were appalled. A delegation from the Virginia Institute of Marine Sciences (VIMS) came to the Conservancy looking for help. Pat Noonan met with them. He, like most people, knew little about Virginia's Eastern Shore. They insisted on telling him everything. They unrolled a large multicolored map of the archipelago that runs from Lewes, Delaware, to Cape Charles, Virginia. It covered the entire conference table.

The upper quarter of the map was crosshatched in red. "The area from Lewes to Ocean City is almost totally developed," the biologists told Pat. "It's gone." The next quarter was crosshatched in green, and covered the area south to Chincoteague. "That's Assateague Island, which is part of the Assateague National Seashore," the biologists explained. "That area is pretty well protected." The bottom half was crosshatched in yellow. "These are the Virginia Barrier Islands. They have flat, wide beaches. They cannot withstand any development. They are our last nesting sites for colonial shore birds."

Here the biologists produced a picture captioned "Royal Terns." It showed thousands of birds milling around on a beach.

"Colonial shore birds nest in colonies. They lay their eggs right on the beaches. As you can see, they could never survive the onslaught of people, especially during the summer, when the chicks are most vulnerable. These birds need isolation, and the Virginia Barrier Islands are their only remaining habitat."

Pat glanced at the picture and began studying the map. He could see that the Virginia Barrier Islands were ripe for development. Plus, he knew that the Bay Bridge Tunnel, which had opened in 1961, was in financial trouble. There were rumors that the Bay Bridge Tunnel Authority might default on its bonds. A default on these bonds would not be good for the commonwealth. A new bridge to the islands would not only please the beachgoers, it would generate more revenue for the Bay Bridge Tunnel. It was easy to understand why the politicians favored development.

Pat was convinced, but he couldn't turn the biologists off. They went on and on. They wanted Pat to know that the marsh served as a breeding ground and nursery for all kinds of marine life. They wanted him to know that the islands were a nesting place for migrating waterfowl, a haven for mammalian wildlife, and the key component of a vital, enormously productive but fast-disappearing ecosystem.

Pat had heard more than enough, but just when he thought they were through, the biologists started talking about storms. They told Pat how the beaches were continually moving, how the winds and waves from thirty northeasters a year moved dunes, closed inlets, and constantly resculpted "these islands of life."

"A road anywhere through the islands would require constant

maintenance just to withstand the northeasters," the biologists said. "When a hurricane comes, and they do come, manmade structures cannot survive."

All during the seventies Pat attacked the Virginia Barrier Islands with more force than any hurricane. He was then president of the Conservancy, and, as director of land acquisition, I followed behind and picked up the pieces. The Conservancy's whirlwind acquisition efforts blew away the developer's plans for a new Ocean City. Once the Conservancy gained control of the islands, the assembly scrapped all proposals for roads and bridges. Any good politician could see the reserve's ecological significance, and given the public's growing interest in the environment, more preserves meant more wildlife, which meant more votes.

Pat felt he'd done everything that the biologists from VIMS had asked. Then they came back for another visit. Pat was sure they wanted to thank the Conservancy for saving the islands. Instead, they produced their large, multicolored map of the archipelago. Now the islands were green, but the marsh and mainland were covered by yellow crosshatching. "Saving the island was only half of the problem," they told Pat. "Now the marshes are threatened by development from the mainland. The Conservancy must protect the mainland."

Dr. Bob Jenkins, the Conservancy's top scientist and most vocal proponent of preserving entire biological systems, quickly concurred. "You've only got half a loaf," Doc told Pat. "Bad business. If we lose the mainland, we lose the whole reserve. All of our work will have been for naught. We must protect the mainland. Remember, bigger is better!"

Bigger was also a lot more expensive. Fully protecting the mainland could easily cost $100 million, or ten times as much as we had sunk into the islands. Acquiring the whole Eastern Shore was out of the question; there had to be a cheaper way.

The more Pat pondered the problem, the clearer the solution became. There were only six deepwater frontages along the entire Eastern Shore. Pat reasoned that whoever controlled these six deepwater frontages controlled development. "No developer's going to invest a lot of money for frontage on the Eastern Shore if he can't get access to the beaches," Pat told me. "Without deepwater frontage, all you've got is farmland. And we can afford to protect farmland."

In the summer of 1980 Pat resigned as president and became a consultant to the Conservancy. He continued to focus his attention on protecting the mainland of the Eastern Shore. By the end of 1984, Pat had orchestrated the Conservancy's acquisition of over 12,000 acres surrounding the six deepwater frontages. We now controlled the most developable land on the Eastern Shore. The biologists from VIMS were ecstatic. Even Dr. Bob was satisfied, which was as close to ecstasy as he ever got. The rest of the Conservancy was nervous. We had invested close to $25 million, the bulk of our permanent capital, into this one preserve.

"Don't worry," Pat told us. "The VCR will make an excellent U.S. Fish and Wildlife refuge. You can sell it to the Feds and get all of your money back."

It would make an excellent Fish and Wildlife refuge, and if we sold it, we would get all of our money back—but by 1984, the Reagan administration, led by Secretary of the Interior James Watt, had made it quite clear that it was not going to create any new wildlife refuges.

It was obvious that we needed a new source of funding. It came, just before Christmas, in the unlikely form of a bald, bespectacled estate lawyer from Cleveland. This lawyer was the principal creator and promoter of an innovative new technique of charitable giving. It was known as the "charitable lead trust."

He wandered into the office one afternoon. He was not a conservationist. The closest he came to nature was when his tee shot strayed into the woods. He wanted to see whoever was in charge of real estate. That was me.

I ushered him into the conference room. I couldn't believe our good luck. He claimed to control millions of dollars, and he wanted to work with the Conservancy. "The ideal investment for a charitable lead trust," the lawyer told me, "is unimproved real estate that will experience strong appreciation over the life of the trust. We are not interested in income-producing assets, because we'd have to give most of the income away. Appreciation, on the other hand, can be passed on to the beneficiary tax-free, plus we can use it to satisfy our distribution requirements."

"But why do you need the Conservancy?" I asked.

"Simple," the lawyer responded. "The trust has to give something to charity every year. The beneficiary is interested in conservation. Rather than give hard cash, I would like to satisfy our payout requirements by buying land, letting it appreciate, and then donating the appreciated real estate."

I was confused. "Come again?"

The lawyer had a little voice that got squeakier when he was exasperated. He started to squeak. He must have assumed that anyone who worked for a charity would understand a charitable lead trust. "Certainly you understand the principle behind a charitable *remainder* trust?" he said, as if talking to some dimwit.

"Sure," I said, trying not to sound too stupid. "An individual transfers assets into a trust tax-free, then the assigns get the income from the trust for *x* number of years. When the trust expires, the assets, or the remainder, are given to some charity. We've done a couple of those."

"Close enough," the lawyer said. "A charitable lead trust works on the same principle. It simply flips the assigns and the charity. In other words, the charity leads by getting the income during the life of the trust. When the trust expires, the assets go to the assigns." Here he paused and smiled. "Tax-free, of course. It's a wonderful way to pass on money."

"I see," I said. "But what do you want from us?"

"Land," the lawyer said. "Say you've got some property that you've bought for conservation, but you think that in a few years it might be very valuable for development. You sell it to the trust for its fair market value. We'll hold it for a few years while it appreciates. We might even help it appreciate by getting it rezoned. Once we've gotten the value we want, we'll give it to some nonprofit for conservation. You get your money. We get a nice donation, and the land stays protected. What do you think?"

"I think it's great," I said, "but we couldn't sell you a truly significant nature area. Our supporters would never understand. It would have to be some land that we bought to buffer a preserve. Something that's not an attractive fundraiser." I looked at the wall. There was the map of the VCR.

"Excuse me while I make a call." I sprinted back to my office, called Pat, and explained the situation.

He immediately grasped the potential. "Let's take him to the Shore on the next full moon. We can't sell the islands, but the farms would be perfect." I looked at my calendar. That would be the second week in January.

I ran back to the conference room. "You want to go to the Virginia Eastern Shore?" I asked.

"Wonderful!" said the lawyer. "I like coastal property. Good appreciation. Everybody wants a place at the beach."

"How are we going to sell the Eastern Shore in January?" I asked Pat, after the lawyer had left.

"Don't worry," he assured me. "I'll arrange a duck hunt. We'll have a great time."

"Oh, no," I moaned, "not another duck hunt."

Pat's last duck hunt to the Eastern Shore had been a near disaster. In 1979, Pat had invited Cecil Andrus, Jim Watt's predecessor, on a duck hunt to the Eastern Shore. Pat figured that this would be a great way to generate some interest in a new National Wildlife Refuge. Unbeknownst to Pat, the guide he'd hired to escort the secretary was well known to all the local wardens. This guide had a reputation for shooting over baited blinds, which is highly illegal. Fortunately, the director of the Fish and Wildlife Service was a good friend of Pat and knew all about hunting on the Eastern Shore. He phoned Pat just as he and the secretary were leaving for the airport and told him that hunting on the Eastern Shore with that particular guide was not a good idea. A couple of hours later, the guide was busted in the very blind that Pat and the secretary were supposed to be shooting. Pat could still visualize the headlines in the *Washington Post*: "Secretary of Interior and Prominent Environmentalist Arrested Shooting Over Baited Blind."

Pat's guides for this trip were two local oystermen named Wayne and Ward. Each stood well over six feet and probably tipped the scales at around 280. Their families had been leasing the oyster beds off one of the Conservancy's farms for more than a century. They weren't professional guides, but they had a few blinds out in the marsh and were eager to please Pat, who they assumed was their landlord. Pat had specifically instructed Wayne and Ward that he wanted nothing to do with baited blinds. They told him not to worry; they had a better way of getting ducks.

We arrived at the Shore just after lunch and spent the afternoon touring the farms around the six deep water sites. The lawyer was not impressed. "Where's the beach?" he kept asking. Pat charged ahead undaunted. He was still pitching the farms as we watched a full moon rise over the marsh.

On the morning of the hunt, Pat was up well before dawn. We

were staying in a rustic old farmhouse on the edge of the marsh. The lawyer and I awoke to the aroma of hot coffee, cinnamon rolls, bacon, and eggs. Pat was cooking up a storm.

As I expected, the lawyer had never been hunting. He came down to breakfast in a velour pullover, yellow corduroy slacks, and tasseled loafers. Pat looked at him in amazement. "We're a long way from the first tee," he said. "Let me get you outfitted."

Pat rummaged through the closets and came out with a down-lined camouflage coat. It was huge; it probably belonged to Wayne or Ward. There were no boots. The lawyer would have to hunt in his tasseled loafers. "Don't worry," Pat said, "it'll be nice and dry in the blind."

Wayne and Ward motored up in their boat just as we finished getting the lawyer dressed. Pat, ever courteous, went out and offered them coffee and a couple of cinnamon rolls. "Naw," said Wayne. "Me'n Ward, we'll catch a bite after we get y'awl settled."

We grabbed our guns and flopped into Wayne and Ward's open boat. The boat crunched through a thin layer of ice into the main channel. The cold from the metal seats stung through our pants. Wayne and Ward couldn't take their eyes off the lawyer. All they could see was a mound of camouflage with a pair of steamed-up glasses sticking out at the top and tasseled loafers dangling from the bottom.

Wayne and Ward pulled up to a blind. It was set in the marsh between two guts. "'Bay ducks, mostly bufflehead and goldeneye, like to raft up in these guts," Wayne told us as we unloaded. "Once y'awl get started, Ward and me'll go up there and start oysterin'. When we move in, them ducks will move out. You shoot 'em when they come by."

"You sure that's legal?" Pat said, "I don't want any rallying." Rallying is the term used for chasing ducks with a boat. I was impressed that Pat knew it. He had learned his lesson well.

"Course it's legal," Ward growled. "Ain't no law 'genst oysterin'."

The first bunch came by, low and fast. The lawyer never saw them. He was making some arcane point about imputed interest rates as they pertained to charitable lead trusts. The second batch turned into the sun before he could shoot. Pat started to fidget. We wanted the lawyer to have the first shot, but we didn't want to run out of ducks.

The lawyer spotted the third group early. He fired. Pat fired. I fired. Down went a duck. "Nice shot," Pat said to the lawyer, winking at me.

"You mean I actually hit one?" the lawyer asked incredulously.

"It was all yours," Pat confirmed. "Quick, reload. Here come some more."

Wayne and Ward were doing a good job "oysterin'." Ducks were streaming down the guts. Bang. Bang. Bang. The lawyer had forgotten all about charitable lead trusts. Every time a duck fell, Pat would give him full credit.

After about an hour, Wayne and Ward came by and picked up the birds. We had a respectable half dozen. "You boys had enough?" asked Ward.

"Yeah, that was great," I said.

"No way," said the lawyer. "Send down some more." Pat looked very pleased. The lawyer was having a great time. "Right," Pat agreed. "Send some more down."

"It'll be a while before they get back into that gut," Wayne said. "Me'n Ward, we're gonna buzz downtown for a quick bite. We'll be back in a coupla minutes. Stay ready. Y'awl might get a few shots as they come back in."

"Okay," I said, "but don't take too long. I'm getting cold."

We waited and waited. No ducks came by. A hard wind had started to blow out of the east. Soon the entire marsh was under water. Pat and I watched as the bay began climbing up the side of the blind. The lawyer didn't seem to notice. He continued to peer out over the edge of the blind, eagerly clutching his gun. The water began lapping through the floorboards. Pat looked at his watch. "What time is high tide?" he asked nervously.

"I don't know," I said. "But we've got a full moon, and that wind has to be pushing in a lot of water." We both looked at the shore. It was a good quarter of a mile away.

"Hey," squeaked the lawyer, "my feet are getting wet."

"Stand on the seat," Pat told him.

"But then the ducks might see me."

"Not in that coat," Pat said. "*We* can't even see you."

By now, the water was over the floor. Soon it would be over the rubber bottoms of our boots. "Push over," Pat told the lawyer. "We're coming up." Pat and I weren't in Wayne and Ward's class, but we certainly weren't lightweights. When we got on the bench, it cracked. We jumped down. Our guns slipped off the seat and fell to the bottom of the blind. The icy water filled my boots.

Suddenly, I couldn't see a thing. The lawyer had draped himself around my neck. "Aaugh! You're choking me!" I croaked.

"Here! Get up on Dave's shoulders," Pat said as he pushed the enormous down jacket over my head. The lawyer had to be in there somewhere. I could feel him twisting and turning. Eventually, the lawyer ended up sitting high and dry on my shoulders, and I had a tasseled loafer in each hand.

"Where's my gun?" he squeaked. "Here comes a duck."

"The hell with the duck. Do you see Wayne and Ward?" I said.

"Yeah, they're right behind the duck," Pat said. He sounded very amused. With Wayne and Ward in sight, he could afford to laugh at me.

"Well, wave them over," I shouted.

I could feel the lawyer waving. "What's happening?" I asked.

"They waved back," Pat said. "They're going up the gut. Here." Pat handed the lawyer a gun. "Get ready."

I couldn't believe it. Pat was going to have the lawyer shoot from my shoulders, and the lawyer was going to do it. Here I was, going numb, while this golfer from Cleveland was still hunting. Pat would do anything to close a deal.

Bang! Bang! I was startled by the shots.

"Holy cow!" exclaimed Pat, genuinely amazed. "You got them both!"

"More shells!" said the lawyer.

"That's it," Pat said. "All the shells are under water." I could tell he was disappointed. I wasn't the least bit disappointed. I could hear a motor approaching. "Ward, will you look at this!" Wayne bellowed. "That water's clean up to their thighs. We ain't had a tide this high in a month a Sunday's."

"How was your snack?" I asked sarcastically.

"Well, we was worried about you, so we cut it short. Ha. Ha. Ha." Ward guffawed. "You wanna go in, or keep shootin'?"

"Get us out of here," I pleaded.

Back at the house, over a stiff drink in front of a warm fire, the lawyer couldn't stop talking about his double. I was trying to get some feeling back in my feet. Pat was loading up for the kill. "Well, what do you think?" he asked the lawyer. "These farms ought to be just right for a charitable lead trust."

"No way," said the lawyer. "I need appreciation. These farms aren't going anywhere. People don't want to look at marsh. They want to walk on the beach."

Pat's jaw hit the floor. I quickly consulted my lunar calendar. I was going to take the lawyer to Dog Island. If he wanted a beach, we'd give him a beach.

For a long time, it looked like the lawyer was right. The real estate market on the Virginia Eastern Shore was dead, but recently, we've been getting calls from local brokers. They tell us that there is a growing demand for farms overlooking the marsh, especially if they have deep water frontage. We think we might be able to recapture some of our funds by restricting the farms from development and selling them to private buyers. We've tried to disguise this new attempt to roll our money by cloaking it in the oxymoron "conservation development." If it works, we'll have conserved the farms and have developed a new source of funds that we can use to buy more land.

As for the lawyer, he stopped promoting charitable lead trusts when Congress shot down most of the tax benefits that could be derived from them. The only time I see his tasseled little feet is when he comes in to kick about the lack of appreciation on Dog Island. I tell him not to worry and quickly switch the conversation to golf.

Absolute Loonacy

MOST OF MY TIME WITH THE CONSERVANCY is spent communing with lawyers and landowners, not nature. My only steady exposure to nature comes every summer, when we go to Maine. We've always gone to Maine for a couple of weeks in July; first to Lovewell Pond in Fryeburg, now to Kezar Lake in Lovell. It was in Maine that I developed my interest in conservation. I've always felt that these lakes are special, and one of the things that makes them special is the loons. In this respect, Kezar Lake is very special.

Kezar, like most lakes in southern Maine, is no longer very wild. It suffers from too many cottages (mine included), too many people, too many big boats, and now even a flotilla of jet-skis, the latest and loudest insult to anything wild. But Kezar does have its loons, and every year they keep coming back.

It has been reported that in all of neighboring New Hampshire, with 156 lakes and ponds, the summer population of loons does not exceed 400. Some days in July, as many as nineteen have been counted on Kezar Lake alone, and in the fall, when they raft up, that number can easily double. One local claimed to have once counted fifty-six swimming in the upper bay, but that figure has never been confirmed. I do know that we have one pair down at our end of the lake, and their eerie calls at all hours of the night give Kezar at least a semblance of wilderness.

Most people in Lovell are very proud of the lake and want to protect what's left of its natural beauty. The Kezar Lake Association is very active. Every year it distributes a brochure outlining the *do*'s and *don't*s of Kezar Lake. The loons are responsible for a lot of the *don't*s. Don't chase them, don't harm them, don't disturb them, don't interfere with them, and don't bother them in any other way.

A well-known story is that when Hollywood came to the Northeast looking for a place to shoot *On Golden Pond,* their first choice was Kezar Lake. But the Kezar Lake Association didn't want anybody upsetting its loons, so Hollywood had to settle for Squam Lake in New Hampshire.

The pair down at our end of the lake often feeds in front of our cabin. I was somewhat surprised one afternoon when my wife suddenly called, "David, come quick! Look at the loons!" I rushed out onto the porch and saw something thrashing about in the brush right at the shoreline. I'd never seen a loon in that close, and what made it even more amazing was that my neighbors, Andy and Marge Koop, were out swimming not thirty feet away. Wild loons just don't get that close to people, not even people as nice as the Koops.

Our son was out on our dock working on his boat. I yelled to him, "Hey, Donald! Look at the loons." If he saw them, he didn't seem to care. "Yeah, sure. Can you bring me down a wrench?"

The loons started to shriek. The Koops stopped swimming. My first thought was the the loons had cornered an exceptionally large and tasty school of fish. What else could make them come so close to humans and the shore? What a break. Here was nature at my very doorstep. I felt privileged to be able to share this unique moment with my family. "Dammit, Don, stop fooling with your boat and look at the loons!"

Don was fifteen, and nature was not on the top of his communing list. He remained preoccupied with his boat. "Dad, you could probably see them a lot better from down here. And when you come, how about bringing me a wrench?"

Don was right. I was too far away. I ran to the dock, without the wrench. When I got there, I saw two loons dive not more than twenty feet from me. While I stared at the cove waiting for them to surface, two streams of air bubbles came streaking under the dock. The loons popped up on the far side of Don's boat. They weren't fishing. They were trying to kill each other. The larger one had the smaller one by the neck and was forcing its head under the water. I could see blood.

Don finally looked up. "Hey, Dad, what are you going to do?"

I didn't know what to do. I couldn't just stand there and watch one loon kill another. On the other hand, was it right to interfere with nature? Survival of the fittest, and all that good stuff? What would the Kezar Lake Association say? I made a quick decision. To hell with Darwin, I didn't want this loon hanging on my conscience.

I leaped off the dock into the shallows. The aggressor saw me coming and released his grip for an instant. That was all the little guy needed. He burst free and beat his way around the point. The big guy took off after him. Both were screaming. I stood there, scared and confused. I felt like the first person at the scene of a horrible accident.

The lots on the points are undeveloped and the shoreline is still well hidden by bushes and trees. I sloshed out of the water through the undergrowth toward the sound of more thrashing, splashing, and screaming. I stumbled over a boulder, and there, at the water's edge directly at my feet were the two loons. The big one again had the smaller bird's neck in his beak and was forcing its head under the water. Again, I didn't know what to do. I could have bent over and pulled them apart, but up this close, these loons looked very big, and the bigger one looked very mean.

I leaned over and waved my arms to signal a TKO and said, "All right, you guys, break it up!" Remarkably, the big loon let go and paddled back to a neutral corner. I expected the little guy to make another break for freedom, but instead—and I swear that this is the truth—he waddled behind my legs and cowered into the bank. I have probably read more articles about loons than there are loons, at least on Kezar Lake, but nothing I have ever read prepared me for this situation. Here I was, standing on the shoreline with one loon howling at me from not more than ten feet away, while the other one, a completely wild bird, hid right behind me. I could have picked him up without taking a step.

Now what? It was obvious that the larger loon wasn't going to quit, and the other one wasn't about to leave my protection. I wasn't about to pick up the smaller bird, which wasn't all that small. The only solution seemed to be to drive the big guy away. But how? Yelling might further upset the bird at my feet. Maybe I could throw some pebbles at him. But there weren't any pebbles, only rocks the size of my head. Those would never do.

Then I remembered Don. "Hey, Donald, get your boat over here, quick!"

"I can't. Where's the wrench?"

That wasn't what I wanted to hear. "Get that boat over here right now, or I'll wrench you."

After what sounded like some muffled unpleasantries, I heard his motor start. He came chugging around the point. When he saw my predicament, even Don was impressed. "Gee, Dad, how did you get so close to that loon?"

"I didn't get close to him. He got close to me. Now get your boat in here and back this other one off." I must have sounded pretty authoritative, because Don gave me one of his infrequent *Yes, sir*'s and slowly nosed his boat between me and the larger loon. The bird turned away from shore, and Don gently herded him down the lake.

With the big bird out of the way, I turned my attention to the poor guy nestled at my feet. Its head was hidden in a clump of grass. I could see the cut on its neck. It wasn't too bad. The loon was breathing heavily, but it seemed all right. I figured the best thing to do was just to leave it alone for half an hour and see what happened. If it hadn't moved by then, I'd call somebody from the Kezar Lake Association.

As I made my way back to the cabin, I was very pleased with myself. I had saved a loon from certain destruction. What more could a conservationist ask of himself?

This good feeling was positively reinforced when I saw an attractive young woman in an equally attractive bikini standing outside my porch. Ah, I thought, no good deed goes unrewarded.

I was wrong. In her hand, the young woman held a Kezar Lake Association brochure, and before I could introduce myself, she said, accusingly, "Is that your son out there in that boat?"

"Yes."

She continued, "Then I am citing you for harassing a loon. We have very strict rules about that here at Kezar Lake."

Citing? I was flabbergasted. Here I was, expecting the Order of Audubon, and I end up getting cited, whatever that meant. "Citing? Me? Miss, I don't think you understand. I just saved a loon. One was trying to kill the other."

She was not convinced. "I saw those two loons. They came right by my beach. They were mating."

Mating? I thought to myself, if this is her idea of sex, I'm glad I'm middle-aged and married. But I didn't say that. What I did say was, "Mating? The mating season's long gone. Those two loons were having a territorial battle."

At this point, my wife, who was still on the porch watching this fiasco, rose to my defense. "He's right," she said. "He helped finance a loon study."

The "he" she was referring to was not me personally, but The Nature Conservancy. In 1984, the Conservancy financed the study of a massive loon die-off (at least five hundred birds) around Dog Island. Since this debate was still up in the air, my wife wisely omitted any mention of the Conservancy. One citation was enough.

The young woman hesitated. I knew that I had her. I quickly pressed my advantage. "I sincerely appreciate your concern, but I think I have the situation pretty well under control. I am letting one loon rest in the weeds over there, and I think that my son has the other one far enough away so that it will no longer be a problem."

It worked. Much to my relief, she seemed satisfied. We moved on into introductions and who-do-you-knows. It turned out that we had bought our canoe from her father twenty years earlier. After a very friendly discussion, she departed with her brochure. I went back and was further relieved to find out that the loon I had saved had regained its composure and returned to the wild.

The next day, I attended the dedication of a virgin forest in northern New Hampshire given to the Conservancy by Champion International. By chance, Tudor Richards, president of the New Hampshire Audubon Society and a recognized expert on loons, was on the speaker's platform with me. After the ceremony, I pulled Tudor aside and told him my story. At its conclusion, I asked him, "Well, Tudor, was I right?" Tudor put on a wistful look and said, "I would have given anything to be there. Astonishing. You didn't by any chance take a picture, did you?"

I was vindicated. But still, I think I'll stick to lawyers and landowners and leave the loons to Tudor Richards and the Kezar Lake Association.

My First Russian

WILBUR E. GARRETT SEEMS TO KNOW something about everything. Besides being the editor of *National Geographic,* Bill is a writer and photographer. His hobbies include archaeology, astronomy, horticulture, woodworking, and tinkering with all kinds of machines. Despite two gimpy ankles, Bill still plays a pretty good game of tennis. He has enough slices and chops to dink me to death.

In my view, Bill's best hobby is his vineyard. For some thirty years, Bill and his wife, Lucy, have grown their own grapes and bottled their own wine under the Patomack label. Theirs may be one of the first vineyards in Virginia to make European-style wine since Thomas Jefferson's. It produces good stuff, much better than the rotgut I usually buy.

While I'm continually amazed by Bill's knowledge, Bill sees nothing unusual about having so many interests. Once, when I complimented him on being a twentieth-century Thomas Jefferson, he thought for a while and said matter-of-factly, "Jefferson never played semi-pro baseball."

I like hanging around with Bill. I never have to say anything. I just listen. He has the inside scoop on all sorts of famous people: Admiral Peary ("definitely reached the North Pole"), Fidel Castro ("just chews his cigars; he quit smoking to set an example for his people"), Noriega ("will leave the nuncio when he runs out of coke"). One of Bill's best stories is about Christopher Columbus. He finds it amusing that Columbus, after stealing the clothes of some peaceful Mayans who had come out to greet him, noted in his diary that he was sure the Mayans would make good Christians because they modestly tried to cover their privates.

I met Bill in the spring of 1988. He had just joined the board of The Nature Conservancy. The leadership of the *National Geographic Society* was becoming more and more concerned about the environment. In January of 1988, as part of its centennial, the Society hosted a symposium on global prospects. The two dozen distinguished scholars who participated were unanimous in their call for "restoration of environmental balance to Planet Earth." Gil Grosvenor, president of the Society, summed up the symposium by declaring that while the *National Geographic*'s first century had been dedicated to a better understanding of the world, its second century would have the added imperative to "encourage a better stewardship of the planet."

Following up on this commitment, Bill devoted *Geographic*'s whole centennial issue (December 1988) to the environment. In most subsequent issues, he would include at least one article on the threats facing some critical natural area. Bill was the first editor of a major publication to publicly recognize that the environment would be the issue of the nineties.

Bill happens to be a neighbor. I've gotten into the habit of dropping by his place on Saturday afternoons. He is always looking for help with some project, and he rewards his workers with plenty of good homegrown European-style wine. One Saturday afternoon, Bill confided in me that he had a plan for conservation. "What we should do," he said, "is get UNESCO, or whatever group is most respected internationally, to designate certain areas as international biospheres."

"The Society," he continued, "could feature these areas in its magazine, films, and books. Then the Conservancy, working with local groups, governmental agencies, and other organizations, could save them."

It made sense to me. During the late seventies we had done a series of major projects. In the early eighties we had undertaken the Rivers of the Deep South. By 1990 we would have completed the National Wetlands Program. A partnership with UNESCO and the *National Geographic* would be a logical step in our protection plans and could raise the Conservancy's land conservation efforts to a new level of effectiveness.

Unlike most environmentalists, Bill does not have preconceived notions of right and wrong. Bill approaches the environment as a journalist; he just wants the facts. He refuses to let the *Geographic* become a blind advocate for any cause. Long before it became obvious, Bill was pointing out that Exxon was wasting an awful lot of money in the process of cleaning up the spill in Prince William Sound. He suspected that Exxon was more concerned with appeasing wild-eyed environmentalists than with addressing the real problems. According to Bill, some of Exxon's cleanup efforts actually made things worse. Steam-cleaning the beaches probably killed every microorganism that had survived the oil. Using Pampers to soak up the crude made great press, but there was no place in Alaska's fragile ecology to dispose of 50,000 tons of oily diapers.

Bill maintained that nature would have taken care of much of the problem. "If the environmentalists had been smart," he said, "they would have told Exxon to forget the P.R. ploys . . . and use that billion to set up a trust fund that would buy more land." Bill feels that the best way to protect an area is to buy it. That's why he likes the Conservancy.

I'm always looking for some way to show our gratitude to Bill for all that he's doing for the Conservancy and conservation. It's not easy. What can you do for a guy who's been just about everywhere and done just about everything? A trip to a Conservancy preserve would be anticlimactic. He has already traveled over most of the world. There's no more room on his walls for testimonials and plaques. Two new ankles are all Bill really wants, but I can't give him those.

In June of 1988, Bill called, needing a favor. He wanted to know whether his property had any ecological significance. His land drops steeply to the Potomac River, and this type of transition zone often harbors rare and endangered plant species. Bill had carefully walked the land and hadn't found anything unusual, but before he cleared out some underbrush, he wanted to make sure. "No problem," I assured him. "I've got just the guy. I'll bring him over."

It sounded like a job for Walt Matia. Walt, though a full generation younger than Bill, is in many ways just as interesting. Besides having been the youngest director of stewardship in the history of the Conservancy, Walt is an accomplished ornithologist, mammalogist, taxidermist, and a superb artist. Walt had just left the Conservancy to see if he could support himself as a wildlife sculptor. After only six months, his bronzes were starting to sell, and sophisticated collectors were becoming interested.

"I wonder if these guys know something I don't," Walt told me with his usual self-deprecation. "Most of them don't really care about my work; I'll bet they're just waiting for me to die. Collectors don't make big money until the artist is dead." Walt would never let success go to his head. I knew Bill would like him.

I arranged a tour of Bill's property for a Friday afternoon; it was

July 1, 1988. I also invited Bill, Lucy, and Walt back to our house for dinner. When Lucy asked whether they could bring anything, I immediately suggested a few bottles of their Patomack wine. It promised to be an enjoyable afternoon and evening.

The morning of July 1, Bill called. He had a slight complication. The editor of the North American desk of *Novosti*, the Russian news agency, was in town. He was an old friend of Bill's; he'd been Bill and Lucy's guide when they were in Russia a few years earlier. He was in Washington trying to promote something called "glasnost." Bill wanted to know if it would be all right to bring him along. "This could be a great opportunity for the Conservancy," Bill told me. "This guy is way up in the Party, and Russia has plenty of environmental problems. If you can sell him on the Conservancy, it might lead to something interesting."

"Bring him along," I said enthusiastically. "We'll feed him the party line. Ha, Ha."

I immediately called my wife. "Let's really lay it on," I told her. "This could be our ticket to Russia."

Our tour left no leaf unturned. Bill, always the journalist, couldn't get enough out of Walt. Walt, always reserved, answered every question but didn't confuse Bill with a lot of extraneous information. Lucy busily traced leaves and took notes. The Russian and I trailed behind. For a Communist, he seemed like a pretty nice guy. His name was Mikhail Derevianko—he told me to call him Mike. I tried to talk with Mike about conservation while we walked along, but there was a stiff breeze blowing. Mike said that he had trouble hearing, that we should wait until we got back indoors.

Walt and I drove back to my house right after the tour. I wanted to make sure that everything was set to sell the Conservancy. Ruth had spared no expense for our first Russian. There were Wisconsin cheeses, Hawaiian nuts, and North Carolina sausage for appetizers. A first course of Maine lobster bisque was to be followed by a big Iowa steak and Idaho potatoes. A cobbler of Georgia peaches would top off this All-American meal. I smacked my lips as I nestled the big Iowa steak on the grill and Walt arranged the Idaho potatoes around it. All that was missing was a tall glass of Patomack wine.

Only Bill didn't bring any Patomack wine. When he and Lucy arrived, they were each carrying a frosty bottle of Russian Stolichnaya, compliments of Mike, who quickly offered the first toast. "To glasnost!"

The truth is that except for an occasional rum and tonic, I try to stay away from hard liquor. I'm a beer and wine man; I tend to get polluted on hard liquor. But I couldn't do anything to insult Mike, my first Russian, and I surely didn't want him to think that conservationists were wine-sipping aristocrats.

I could feel my eyes begin to water as the Stolichnaya burned its way down my gullet. My head began to spin. After several more toasts, it became clear even to my muddled mind that Mike was a firm disciple of this new guy Gorbachev. Judging from the headlines in that morning's *Washington Post,* Russia was undergoing some major changes. I had no idea what glasnost was all about, but according to the *Post*, a delegate at the Soviet Communist Party Conference had called for the ouster of President Andrei Gromyko. That was a real sign of change—Gromyko had been around ever since I could remember.

Bill offered a toast to the "new regime." Always the journalist, he was using the toast to elicit more information. Mike enthusiastically raised his glass, indicating to Bill that there was in fact a new regime. Bill looked at me and winked. Maybe this change would present an opening for the Conservancy and conservation.

I went out to check on the steak while Ruth had Walt elaborate on one of his new pieces, a pair of California quail that I had given Ruth for her birthday. We figured that the quail might be a nice way to lead

Mike into a discussion on conservation. But Mike showed no interest in Walt's quail. He followed me outside. For some reason, he was determined that I should grasp the significance of glasnost. He handed me another Stolichnaya. I figured that it was time for me to do some promoting of my own. Now was the time to confirm our reservations to Russia.

"To conservation," I said, raising my glass with a flourish. Mike politely raised his own glass, but it was clear he hadn't understood me.

"So what's this guy Gorbachev doing for the environment?" I asked.

"Pardon?" Mike said, cupping his left ear.

"The environment!" I shouted. "What's Gorbachev doing for the environment!"

"Ah, environment," Mike said. "Gorbachev is very tough on environment. Just other day he caught some officials, high-ranking members of Party, swimming in reservoir outside Moscow. He exposed them immediately!"

I started to laugh: I thought Mike was making some joke about Soviet skinny-dipping. Then I realized he was serious. If this guy Gorbachev's biggest environmental coup was catching some guys swimming in the Moscow reservoir, it made me wonder about the rest of glasnost. Maybe Mike was backing the wrong bear.

Mike must have sensed my lack of enthusiasm. "And what do you do?" he asked. Here, at last, was my opening.

"Oh," I said enthusiastically, "I'm in conservation."

"Whaat?"

"Conservation! I'm in conservation! You know, birds!"

Mike's eyebrows lifted. "Ahh. So you like to look at birds. Verrry nice. We too like birds." He went inside, leaving me to poke my steak. Aeroflot was departing without me.

Once we sat down, Mike rambled on about the Party Congress

while the rest of us slurped our lobster bisque. He was throwing out names like Vladimir Melinkov, Yegor Ligachev, and Boris Nikolaevich as if they lived next door. Bill, and maybe Lucy, were the only ones who knew what he was talking about. I didn't have a clue.

I tried to persuade Walt to tell us a hunting story while Ruth served the meat and potatoes. I remembered once seeing a picture of Brezhnev stalking a wild boar. Maybe hunting was the way to move the conversation into conservation. But Walt was too polite to interrupt Mike.

Ruth's food finally overcame Mike's ideology. There was a break in the conversation while he attacked his meat and potatoes. Bill seized the opportunity. "Dave," he said, "why don't you tell Mike about one of the Conservancy's projects."

I tossed back another Stolichnaya. The stuff was starting to go down like beer. I decided that Mike was far too preoccupied with glasnost to appreciate the intricacies of a Conservancy project. He needed to relax. I had to get him laughing. It was time for "The Pretzel Hold."

"The Pretzel Hold is one of my favorite stories. I've used it on more than one occasion to loosen up a tight social situation. "Mike," I said, "you realize we had our own crisis back in 1973 with Nixon and Watergate. What you probably don't realize is that Nixon turned to Russia to save his presidency!"

Mike, Walt, and Bill all gave me a confused look. Ruth saw what was coming. "While you tell your story, Lucy and I will get dessert." Ruth is one of the few people on earth who knows how to escape the Pretzel Hold.

"Nixon knew that he had to get the country's mind off of Watergate," I continued, "and he figured the best way to do this was to hold a summit with the Russians in Moscow. He had Kissinger set it up. Surprisingly, the Russians agreed, but with one condition. There would have to be a U.S.–Soviet wrestling meet the night before the summit. It was to be held in the Moscow Coliseum." I was rolling. The Stolichnaya had greased my delivery. I described the Coliseum, the crowd, and the wrestlers.

"The meet was tied, four to four, when the heavyweights took the mat. Nixon, Kissinger, Brezhnev, and Gromyko were sitting right at ringside. They knew that whoever took this last match would win the meet and go into the summit with a psychological edge. Grabowski was America's heavyweight. Technically, he was a better wrestler than the Russian, but the Russian had a move called the Pretzel Hold! Nobody had ever broken the Pretzel Hold!"

Here I got up on my feet so I could reenact the match.

"With less than a minute to go, Grabowski was ahead. Nixon was going crazy! Kissinger was going crazy! Sixty million Americans, glued to the tube, were going crazy! Then Grabowski slipped! Before he knew it, the Russian had him in the Pretzel Hold! There was a tremendous cheer from the 14,232 Russians packed into the Moscow Coliseum! Nixon let out a groan! Kissinger let out a groan! Sixty million Americans let out a groan! Nixon's presidency was doomed!" I paused and took yet another shot of Stolichnaya.

"Suddenly, much to everyone's surprise, Grabowski flipped the Russian and pinned him! While Nixon paraded around spreading his fingers in the victory sign, Kissinger grabbed Grabowski. 'How did you do it?' he asked. 'How did you break the Pretzel Hold?'

" 'Geze, Mr. Secretary!' Grabowski said, waving a little American flag for the TV cameras. 'Ya know, when I slipped and da Russian got me in da Pretzel Hold, I felt dis excruciating pain. Den when I opened my eyes, I seen dese two huge testicles sittin' right in front of my face! I tought about da AAU and about da meaning of sportsmanship. Den I tought about you and da president and America, and I figured, what da hell! I opened my mout' and went AAAUURGH!' "

This was the best part of the joke: I opened my mouth, clenched my teeth, shook my head, and went "AAAUURGH," just like I was biting into those two huge testicles. Thanks to the Stolichnaya, I had never done it better.

"Kissinger was intrigued. 'Vat did dat accomplish?' he asked.

" 'Let me tell ya, Mr. Secretary. Ya never know what ya capable of doin' till after you've bitten yaself on da balls!' "

I sat down to join in the laughter. There wasn't any. Walt smiled politely. Bill smiled politely. Mike just sat there with a blank look on his face. He either didn't hear or didn't understand my best joke. I belted down my last Stolichnaya. For the first time in history, the Pretzel Hold had bombed. I wasn't going first class to Russia. I'd be lucky to make coach to Kansas City. I don't even remember the peach cobbler.

I still drop by Bill's on Saturday afternoons for a sampling of Patomack wine. I am pleased to see that Bill has emerged as the leading spokesman for the environment. Almost every issue of the *National Geographic* has at least one article on an area of critical environmental concern. Recent covers have featured a loon, a sea lion, and a pigeon guillemot soaked with oil from the Exxon Valdez spill. The April 1990 issue features the most spectacular photo-essay anyone's ever done on vanishing wildlife. Bill's own story on La Ruta Maya (October 1989) is a blueprint for international conservation. Bill wants to resurrect the Mayan culture as a model for unifying and protecting the natural, archaeological, and cultural heritage of Central America. With forty million readers to back him up, Bill is in a position to do it.

Postscript: On April 16, 1990, Wilbur E. Garrett was summarily fired from the *National Geographic*. His Earth Day editorial (May 1990) accused many self-proclaimed conservationists of being just "conversationists" and challenged politicians, corporations, and concerned individuals to add some action to their words by buying a piece of La Ruta Maya.

It appears that Gil Grosvenor might have bitten himself in a sensitive spot when he fired Bill Garrett. According to a front-page article in the April 17 *Washington Post*, "Sources insisting on anonymity said Garrett and Gilbert M. Grosvenor, scion of the *Geographic*'s founding family, had been on a slow but inevitable collision course over the editor's single-minded efforts to adapt the 102-year-old magazine to a changing, and younger, readership."

I'm not worried about Bill. He's as quick as a cat and will land on his feet when dropped from any height, even with his gimpy ankles. I am worried about the *National Geographic*. It appears that the number-one heavyweight of nonprofit organizations, and potentially the world champion for the environment, may have slipped and fallen into the Pretzel Hold.

Always Grab the Leader

THE GARLANDS WERE, WITHOUT QUESTION, the finest fishermen at Jordan's Camps. They consistently caught more fish than anybody—perch, pickerel, hornpout, and even an occasional bass. Watching them unload their boat was the highlight of an evening at Jordan's. Mr. Garland, a big, heavy-set, good-looking man in a white T-shirt soiled by the flapping of numerous fish, would hold up the pick of the catch and say, "Take a look at this one." Half a dozen flashlights would focus on the fish. Then he'd tell his son, Bobby, "Hand me that one," and immediately another beauty would sparkle in the lights. One night the Garlands came in with an eel. Nobody could figure out what an eel was doing in Lovewell Pond, but if it was there, you could bet that the Garlands would catch it.

The Garlands, Bill, Betty, and Bob, always stayed in Rose Marie, the cabin nearest to the main beach. They liked being right on the water, close to their boat. Mr. Doherty claimed that the reason the Garlands stayed in Rose Marie was because they didn't want to strain themselves carrying all those fish to one of the back cabins. Mr. Doherty was the only guy at Jordan's who didn't care about fishing. He preferred to sit on his porch with a big gin and tonic and comment on the camp as it passed by. There wasn't too much drinking at Jordan's Camps, but Mr. Doherty could get away with it because he was Irish. If it weren't for his family, Mr. Doherty would have been quite content to spend his vacation playing the ponies at Suffolk Downs.

My family always stayed in Little Beaver. Little Beaver was the mirror image of Rose Marie, but it was on the other side of Jordan's Camp. My father liked Little Beaver because it had its own smaller beach, and he could keep our boat right in front of the cabin. This meant that his fish wouldn't have to compete with the Garlands'. Nobody wanted his fish competing with the Garlands'.

Things really got bad in 1955. That was the year the Garlands showed up with an outboard motor, a brand-new three-horsepower Evinrude. Bobby had won it at the Sportsman's Show. His father had entered him in the casting contest. He beat everybody, even the kids in the older age groups. Ted Williams had made the presentation. The February 16 *Boston Herald* featured a picture of Bobby holding the motor, standing between his dad and Ted Williams. None of us could believe it. There were the Garlands with Ted Williams *and* a brand-new motor. It was going to be a long summer.

The Garlands' new mobility only added to their proficiency. They were coming in with bigger catches all the time; plus, with the motor, they could go fish any lake they wanted. When Mr. Garland's brother, Dick, came up for a visit over the Fourth of July, Betty decided to serve the traditional salmon and green peas at the camp's annual cookout. They threw their boat on top of their car and headed for Kezar Lake, where supposedly there were a few landlocked salmon. Nobody at Jordan's had ever dreamed of catching a landlocked salmon. At Jordan's, we traditionally substituted perch, pickerel, hornpout, or an occasional bass for salmon.

That night, my father brought our boat in to the main beach. He had brought in a nice fourteen-inch white perch. All the lights were focused on his fish. We went to bed happy. The next thing I knew, my brother was shaking me, saying, "Get up! Get up! You've gotta see this fish!" There were the Garlands. They were holding the most beautiful fish I had ever seen. It was a landlocked salmon, plump and silvery with a majestic head, and speckled with green and pink dots. They had caught it up at Kezar Lake. My father's fourteen-inch perch looked small and drab by comparison.

At the cookout the next day, we had lots of peas and very modest portions of perch. The Garlands' thick, rosy salmon steaks, slathered with butter and garnished with parsley, dominated the grill. They generously offered to share their salmon, but everyone, except Mr. Doherty, was too proud to accept. Mr. Doherty went back for seconds.

After the cookout, my father took to sleeping on the porch. I would hear him get up with the sun, grab his fishing rod, slip out the door, and row off down the pond. I knew where he was going. Rumor had it that a humongous pickerel lived in the weeds, down by the outlet. My dad just took one lure with him, a Johnson Weedless. He was going after that pickerel.

On the third morning, I got up and offered to join him. "Sure," he said. "I could use the company." It was a glorious Maine morning, cool and clear without a breath of air. Lovewell Pond was perfectly calm. I sat in the bow and looked back into the White Mountains. There was still a trace of snow on Mount Washington. Old Tom, our local eagle, flew over, looking for a school of perch. Normally we'd follow Old Tom anywhere on the pond, but today my father wasn't thinking perch; his thoughts were focused on that humongous pickerel.

It must have been about seven when we reached Rappatuck, the girls' camp near the end of the pond. My father stopped rowing. It was getting warm, and he had broken into a sweat. We listened to reveille being blown—on a real bugle, by a real bugler. I squinted into the sun, hoping to see some nubile young camper sprinting for the shower. We glided by without so much as a glimpse. Maybe Dad's luck would be better than mine.

He let the boat come to rest in the middle of the lily pads and immediately lit up a Camel. It is a wonder that my father is still alive. He was always lighting up Camels, two packs a day. He once tried a Kool, but said that sucking on those filters would give him a hernia. He did enjoy his Camels, and after a couple of hernia-free drags, he snapped the Johnson Weedless onto the end of his leader. The Weedless looked good, even out of the water; a graceful silver spoon, gleaming in the sunlight.

My dad was a great caster. Were it not for the Depression, he probably could have played pro ball. He always said that Ted Williams developed his arm by casting. Ted Williams was our family idol. The Splendid Splinter was a Hall of Fame ballplayer; a Hall of Fame fisherman, never wore a necktie, did whatever he damned well pleased, and was the best at whatever he did. What really bothered us about the Garlands' motor was not the motor itself, but the fact that Ted Williams, our idol, had given it to them.

I watched with pride as the Weedless soared over the bog and plopped into the water a good twenty yards from our boat. Bobby Garland might be accurate, but he'd never have my father's distance. The Weedless wiggled back and forth as it snaked its way through the lily pads. A little bar on the underside kept it from snagging. The bar would depress, exposing the hook, when a fish hit the lure.

The only depression this morning was on our boat. Dad's old reel couldn't handle his powerful arm. He got a backlash on almost every cast.

He was working on a rat's nest when I noticed that his line had gone taut. "Dad, you must have hooked a log," I said. I figured that the

Weedless had sunk to the bottom and a branch had tripped the bar. That was not unusual. Dad stopped, put the rod between his legs, lit up another Camel, and went to work on the reel.

Suddenly, I saw the end of the bog erupt. Lily pads seemed to explode as the white underside of the biggest pickerel I had ever seen twisted and turned over the surface. "Holy mackerel!" my father shouted. "I've got 'im!" Ignoring the backlash, he started to reel in. The thrashing of lily pads and water began to move toward our boat. He had him!

It was my father's finest fifteen minutes. He stood there erect, one foot propped against the gunwald, muscles rippling under his clean white T-shirt, a Camel drooping from his mouth, sweat pouring from his brow, playing that humongous pickerel for all it was worth. Even the Garlands had never brought home a fish this big. The fish put up a tremendous fight. He was giving Dad everything he had, tugging the Weedless all over the bog. Once he even came out of the water. He really was humongous. My dad's old rod was nearly bent in half.

I was sure we were going to lose him when he went under the boat. But Dad scrambled to the stern and quickly guided the line around the keel with his free hand. That was it. The big fish seemed to acknowledge that he had been beaten. He slowly floated to the surface. We could see his whole body for the first time. He had to be at least three feet long.

My father maneuvered the fish to the edge of the boat. "Okay, Davey," he said with finality, "bring him in." We didn't have a net; with all the little stuff we caught, we never needed one. I leaned over, grabbed the line, and hoisted the fish. Just when I got him out of the water, he gave one last little twitch. I could hear my father yelling, "Grab the leader! Grab the leader!" I stood stunned as I watched the line snap. The fish slid back into the water. It just lay there, with its gills pumping for oxygen. The Weedless, the leader, and a couple of feet of line were dangling from its mouth. My father lurched to the side of the boat. He frantically plunged his arm into the water. He was still yelling, "Grab the leader! Always grab the leader!" But he missed it. Dad's humongous pickerel flicked its tail and was gone.

It was a long, silent trip back to camp. I was still in the bow, so I couldn't see my father's face. I was surprised he didn't throw me out after the fish. Thank goodness we could sneak back into our own little beach. I was so mortified I didn't want to see anybody, and I knew that the whole camp would be down at the main beach for a midmorning swim.

Unexpectedly, my father rowed right past Little Beaver. He beached our boat in front of Rose Marie. Everyone came over to see what we had caught. Mr. Doherty was just finishing a salmon croquette. "Well, Jack, now that we've finally polished off the salmon, what have you got for us?"

"We almost had a pickerel, but hc was so big we decided to leave him for the Garlands," Dad said. Suddenly, I couldn't contain myself. I started to spit out the whole story. I was more excited than I would have been if we had caught the fish. Bill Garland wanted to know every detail: where we were, what type of lure we were using, how far Dad cast, how the fish behaved, how Dad kept him from getting tangled under the boat, how I grabbed the line and not the leader. By the time I got through with that pickerel, even Mr. Garland was convinced that Dad had hooked the biggest fish in Lovewell Pond. Dad just sat there, holding the rod with its broken line. He didn't say a word. He didn't need to. He must have known that I'd sell his fish better than he could. And I did. For the rest of the summer, it didn't matter how many fish the Garlands brought in. All everyone wanted to know was whether they had caught Dad's humongous pickerel.

Born and raised in Arlington, Massachusetts, David Morine graduated from Amherst in 1966 and received an MBA from Darden (UVA) Business School in 1969. He worked in recreational real estate development until 1972, when he realized he favored conservation much more than development.

From 1973 to 1988 Morine served as the vice president for land acquisitions for The Nature Conservancy at its national headquarters in Arlington, Virginia. He directed all acquisition efforts and was responsible for completing 5,000 projects that protect more than three million acres of the finest natural areas left in America.